WIN!

A Leader's Guide to

Building a Winning Team

A Leadership Fable

By David Akers

Win!

ISBN: 1-45-287554-5
EAN 13:   978-1-45-287554-5

This publication is designed to provide accurate and authoritative information in regard to the subject matter covered. It is sold with the understanding that neither the author nor the publisher is engaged in rendering legal, accounting, or other professional service. If legal advice or other expert assistance is required, the services of a competent professional person should be sought.

---From a declaration of principles jointly adopted by a Committee of the American Bar Association and a Committee of Publishers.

For information about reproductions, of to inquire about special discounts for bulk purchases, contact Akers Consulting Group, LLC via e-mail at info@AkersConsultingGroup.com

Being a fable, the characters portrayed in the book are fictitious. Any resemblance to actual living persons is coincidental. The lessons provided within are based on true-life experience in developing strong, winning teams. Only the characters are fictional.

Published by Akers Consulting Group, LLC

Printed in the United States of America

Credit where Credit is Due!

This book would not have made it past the first outline if it wasn't for the wonderful support of my family. From my loving wife Lenore and my daughter Kristin, who both put up with me spending the large amount of time it took writing and rewriting this book to make it worthy of your reading. From my sons, Bryan and Danny, who inspire me to always be the best man I can be.

In addition, I'd like to give proper credit to the great friends that helped make this book possible. To Lisa Maggi, for her meticulous editing and for keeping me grounded at all times. To Kevin Zall, who's input I always give the highest level of respect. To Joseph Gordon, who's fresh outlook on things is always a marvel to behold. Also, to Shelley Palma, for taking time out of her busy schedule to provide valuable feedback.

I'd be remised if I didn't also recognize the numerous people I have had the opportunity to work for and with, both the good and the bad. They have given me great insight into what works well and what doesn't, as well as what leadership behaviors can inspire, and which ones can cause a mess.

Thanks must also be given to the numerous men and women who have made up my teams in the past. They were unknowingly both students and teachers in the development and perfection of my approach to building winning teams. I'm happy to say that this approach has been very successful, and I owe these team members a great deal of appreciation for their hard work. It was truly an honor to have the opportunity to lead them.

Introduction

Win-ning [win-ning] **adjective:** that wins; successful or victorious, as in a contest

Team [teem] - **noun:** a number of persons forming one of the sides in a game or contest: a number of persons associated in some joint action

Building and maintaining a true winning team is a difficult task, especially if you have not had the rare opportunity of being mentored by someone that has accomplished this feat.

The following is an imaginary, veracious fable that describes the choice encounter of two men; One that has been placed in a leadership role and desperately needs to build a winning team environment; Another that is arguably one of the best architects of winning teams in the country.

Their choice encounter leads to entertaining conversations on a number of key topics, allowing the new leader to emerge with a newly-found sense of confidence. Can he turn those lessons into actions and lead his team to victory in the marketplace?

At the end of the book, you will find important documents that you can leverage in your quest for building a winning team, but don't peek until you've read through their incredible and entertaining discussions.

Contents

Section 1

Meeting Coach

Section 2

Winning Teams Don't Just Happen

Section 3

A Strategy for Winning

Section 4

Let the Games Begin

Section 5

Important Documents

Section 1

Meeting

Coach

1

Get Me Out Of Here!

Chase Dunning looked down at his watch. The direction of the hands on the watch showed that it was only 2:30 in the afternoon. He let out a long sigh, and pulled the conference agenda out of his portfolio binder. Aside from a few notes he had taken during the morning session, the paper pad within the portfolio was blank. According to the agenda, this session of the conference was scheduled to last another two and a half hours.

He had long since tuned out the current speaker, who was discussing the topic of performance reviews. Not that the topic itself was not of interest to Chase, but the monotone speaker and his boring presentation was driving many of the attendants in the large room to a near state of unconsciousness. Chase had earlier spotted four different typos in the speaker's PowerPoint presentation, which also did not flow very well. Had all of the earlier speakers been better, Chase could feel some level of embarrassment for this speaker. Instead he felt a twinge of anger, not at the speaker, but at the situation he found himself in. Chase looked around the room to see if any of the people were actually engaged. He smiled as he noticed three people who were actually asleep; noted by their heads bobbing up quickly, then slowly retreating back down towards their chests. Many of the people close to Chase were holding their various handheld phones and PDAs down by their knees, busily checking e-mails, playing games, or possibly updating their blogs. Chase noted that several of the chairs that had been occupied earlier, were now empty.

This was not what Chase had expected. He had been eagerly awaiting this conference. The marketing materials had promised an exciting and engaging workshop atmosphere where you would learn "hands on" how to be a great leader. The topics that were to be covered were of great interest to him, and he had hoped to learn a good deal of professional tips and information that he could use in his new leadership position. After less than one full day of the three-day seminar, he was doubting if he would learn anything that would be useful. He had left his wife back in Philadelphia for an entire week, missed an entire week of working at his new job, and perhaps worst of all, he had paid for this seminar with his own money. He clearly had higher expectations than what the speakers were delivering.

Chase had left his blackberry in his hotel room with the thought of not wanting to be distracted. Now how he wished he had brought it with him. He was glad that he had chosen not to sit in one of the front rows. Instead he had selected a chair in the middle of the room, about eleven rows back. There were another five or six rows behind him, but only a dozen or so of those chairs were currently occupied.

The thought of getting up and walking out had crossed Chase's mind several times in the last hour. He mentally wrestled with the idea, trying, yet failing to develop a logical justification to himself for doing so. His mind kept providing him with reasons to stay. He had spent good money to be there, so missing part of it would be like throwing money away. It would be rude to leave, as he wouldn't want anyone to walk out on his meetings. Perhaps it was going to get better in a few moments. The next speaker will be much better.

At 2:45, the un-engaging speaker called for a short break, asking everyone to be back in fifteen minutes to start back up. The relieved audience quickly headed for the exit doors. Chase scooped up his seminar binder and portfolio and joined the group as they anxiously left the meeting room. Chase followed several of the men into the restroom, where the group was very candidly expressing their disappointment in the day's sessions. Two of the men stated that they weren't heading back in, and that they would rather head to the beach than suffer through two more hours of the mind-numbing sessions.

Chase had natural leadership skills, and was not considered to be much of a follower, but in this case he decided to join in the two men's idea of skipping the remaining two hours. Chase wasn't too keen on heading to the beach at the moment; heading over to the lounge was more of his style. He exited the restroom and headed off to his hotel room. As he walked towards the elevator, he recalled opening the door to his room after checking in the night before. The flight in had been smooth and non-eventful; his luggage had arrived; and his hotel room was spacious and offered great views of the ocean and the large pool. He had been sure that these were all signs that the week was going to be fantastic. The day's sessions had quickly brought him back to reality.

Chase decided not to change clothes, and eagerly brushed his teeth - still having the garlic taste of the lunch salad dressing in his mouth. He hadn't had the opportunity to explore the resort the night before, and had gone straight to the conference center first thing this morning, so he wasn't sure where a good bar was located on the property. He could see the building that served as the poolside cabana and restaurant from his window, so he decided to head there first to check it out. He left his seminar materials behind, grabbed his blackberry and hotel key card, then headed down the hallway towards the elevators. As the elevator door opened for him, he stepped in and joined a gentleman whom he recognized from the seminar audience. Chase noticed that the man was still carrying his seminar binder.

"Heading back in for more?" Chase asked.

"Yeah, hasn't been too great yet, but I'm hoping it's going to get better," the man answered. "What about you?"

"Nah, I've had enough for one day," Chase replied honestly. "Think I'll head down by the pool and enjoy the sunshine and great weather."

"I don't blame you. My company sends me to sessions like this every year. I look at them as a vacation. They're usually held in nice locations, and I don't mind suffering through some boring speakers. Though sometimes they are really good. "

The elevator opened on the main floor and both men stepped out.

"Have fun," Chase told the man as they exited and headed in opposite directions down the hallway. Chase heard the man reply "Thanks, you too."

As Chase walked down the interior hallway towards the pool area, he thought about what the man in the elevator had just said. He just couldn't see himself coming to sessions like this every year. He would feel like a failure if he needed to come every single year in order to gain the leadership skills necessary for his current position, or any other. In reality, if he couldn't get things under control and heading in the right direction soon, he most likely wouldn't have his current job much longer. This thought soured his mood even more. He needed to figure things out quickly, and he had no faith that the seminar he was here to attend was going to provide him the information he was desperately seeking.

Stepping out of the building into the bright sun, he was mad at himself for not grabbing his sunglasses. He squinted his eyes, and placed his right hand across his forehead as a visor. He walked past the pool and the good number of people that were occupying the lounge chairs, baking themselves to a nice rosy shade of red while sipping on their large tropical drinks. He stepped inside the building that served as the poolside bar. It was designed and decorated to give you the illusion of being in a remote tropical setting, with a long wooden bar, support columns that were shaped like oversized tiki-idols, thatched grass covering the inside of the ceiling, and reggae music playing through the speakers. As a more modern and urban comfort to the clientele, two flat screen televisions were mounted behind the bar, tuned to the all-day sports channels.

Chase blinked his eyes as he walked towards the bar. The bright sun was still playing havoc on his sight, with large spots jumping around in front of him. At this time of day, the tropical retreat was not very busy. There were three ladies seated together at one of the tables. They were heavily engaged in a conversation amongst themselves. A waitress, dressed in a bright blue tropical shirt had just delivered a fresh round of large tropical drinks to the women. The other tables were currently empty. At the bar, there were only two single men seated. There were three empty stools between the two men. Chase walked up to the bar and sat in the middle of the three empty stools, allowing one empty stool between himself and each of the other men. The bartender was a large Polynesian male, dressed in a bright orange Hawaiian shirt. He quickly came over to Chase and welcomed him in a very friendly voice, "Hey man, welcome to The Oasis. What can I get for you?"

"I'll start with whatever light beer you have on tap," Chase answered, noticing that the man's nametag identified him as "Big Joe".

"Coming right up," Big Joe replied as he grabbed an empty glass and started pouring the requested beverage. "You want to start a tab?"

"Sounds like a good plan." Chase's attitude was already getting better. Perhaps it was the atmosphere, or it was the feeling of not having to listen to another boring speaker today.

"What brings you here, business or pleasure?" Big Joe asked as he placed Chase's drink in front of him.

"Work, but so far it hasn't been very pleasurable."

"Oh man, that's not cool. This is a relaxing and peaceful place. People come here to wind down. Sounds like you aren't off to a good start."

"Don't get me wrong, the place is nice. It's just that I came here for a leadership conference hoping to learn some great new ways of leading my team, but so far the meetings have been terrible. I dropped a good amount of cash, and I'm worried that I'm not going to get anything from it. But hey, I'm venting. Sorry about that," Chase commented.

"No worries. Here's some free pretzels to help turn your day around," Big Joe offered as he slid a bowl in front of Chase.

"Thanks Joe"

"It's Big Joe!", he replied with a smile on his face as he pointed towards the nametag on his bright shirt.

"Sorry, thanks Big Joe," Chase corrected. Big Joe's positive attitude seemed to wear off on him a little. He felt better, but not sure exactly why.

Chase turned to his right and raised his glass in a welcoming gesture as he made eye contact with the man. "How you doin'?" Chase offered as an icebreaker. The man did the same with his glass and replied, "Can't complain." This man looked quite a few years older than Chase, but the man seemed to have a presence about him. Chase noticed that he had a good, strong voice, and a very clean and professional image about him, right down to the clothes he was wearing. While the sunspots in his eyes had not completely cleared up, he thought that the man looked somewhat familiar. Chase turned his head back towards the bar.

Chase watched the two televisions, quickly getting the top headlines in the sports world. He glanced at the gentleman sitting to his left, who was currently speaking to Big Joe. The man was easily in his seventies, and Chase picked up from the conversation between the bartender and the man that he was here with his wife, who was currently out shopping for clothes that she really didn't need, but felt that she had to have.

"You've got to be kidding me," Chase heard the gentleman to his right mumble. Chase turned to see the man staring at the flat screen mounted to their right. Chase focused on the screen, which showed the familiar layout of the announcer with a photo of the person they were speaking about in the upper right corner of the screen. The volume on the television was turned off, so the announcer's words were visible via the closed captioning. The announcer was in the middle of a story regarding a particular professional sports team, who had won the championship the month prior.

Chase immediately understood why the man had made the comment, as the face in the photo was identical to the man sitting right next to him. Chase knew he had looked familiar, but couldn't believe that he was sitting next to the coach that had just recently led the Philadelphia team to its first championship in over two decades. He had won his third championship overall, the first person to ever lead two different teams to that level. Chase decided to continue reading the words of the sports news reporter and understand why his neighbor at the bar was being discussed.

The reporter continued, "Coach Billings exceeded everyone's expectations by leading the underdog Philadelphia team to their first championship. The question is now, what will Coach Billings do next? Will he stay on as the coach, or will he leave the sport while he's on top? If he did, Coach Billings' legacy would continue, as four other coaches in the league came out of his program. According to sources close to Billings, the coach will announce his decision later this month." The station broke for a commercial.

Chase wasn't sure what the proper etiquette was in these situations. He had never been so close to a person of such fame. Should he not say anything and let the man drink in peace, or would it be ok for him to start a conversation with the man? Chase's fears were swept away when Coach Billings turned to him and said, "Can you believe that? Where do they get this stuff, and where to they get off spreading it all over the news?

Chase replied, "I don't know. Are you saying that the story isn't true?"

"That's exactly what I'm saying. I have no thoughts of leaving my job. I worked hard to build a winning team, and why would I walk away from that now? By the way, my name is Don, Don Billings, but everyone calls me Coach." he said as he extended his hand towards Chase.

Chase grasped the coach's hand firmly and replied, "I'm Chase Dunning. It's a pleasure to meet you. I've been to a few games and am a big fan of yours."

"Nice to meet you Chase. What brings you here?"

"I'm here for a leadership seminar. Today was the first day, and I ducked out early because, quite frankly, it wasn't what I was expecting. It runs for two more days, so I'm really hoping it gets better soon," Chase explained.

"I overheard you telling our big friend over there," pointing over at Big Joe. "What's the problem with the seminar? I saw their posters up all around the resort. Looks like a professional gig."

"Yeah, well that's what I was expecting, but it hasn't turned out to be very good so far," Chase replied.

"Expectations can get in the way of success," Coach Billings offered. "Why don't you scoot down a chair here so that we can talk without having to raise our voices."

"Thanks Coach, but I don't want to intrude," Chase explained, sheepishly hoping that Billings would want to continue talking.

"It's no intrusion, after all I'm the one that offered. I've often wondered what goes on in those leadership seminar meetings. I've been asked to speak at them, but it's never worked out with my schedule. I don't get much down time from my job, in fact this is one of the few weeks that I don't spend time at the office, on the phone, or in meetings. My wife demands that I take a week each year, to go somewhere like this, and just unwind."

Chase slid his glass down the bar as he moved one stool over and was now sitting next to one of the most respected sports figures in the country.

"Ok Chase, now tell me why you think you need to attend this meeting, and what you were expecting from it."

2

An Offer Too Good to Refuse

Chase started explaining to Coach Billings the recent events that led to Chase attending the leadership conference.

"I've held several different management positions in my career. I've done pretty well in those positions, and have made a good name for myself, but I realize that in those situations, I had it pretty easy. The team culture was already in existence, and I was following someone else's lead. Someone else had set the vision and put the policies in place. All I needed to do was to execute their plan. I also inherited some pretty good teams, and I know now how good I had it walking into a situation like that. I only needed to keep everyone happy and the numbers were good."

"That's definitely not the case in my new position," Chase continued. " I attended a great university, have a solid resume, and thought I was ready to take the next step and really lead a company. I interviewed and landed a great position with this promising organization. They hired me to build and lead their organization. I quickly realized that I was in over my head in regards to developing a strategy to build a team environment. I think I have some great ideas, but there is so much to do, and I'm worried that it will been tough getting everyone on board. I don't really have anyone to go for help, and I came here hoping to learn some great tricks to use."

"You realize that true leadership is not about tricks, right?" Coach Billings asked.

"Maybe tricks isn't the right word, but I really need some help figuring out how to lead this organization. I've never failed in anything, and I don't intend to start now," Chase responded.

"Perhaps I could give you a few pointers," Billings offered.

"Thanks for the offer, and I surely don't mean any disrespect, but I'm not sure that your background aligns with my situation. You coach teams, and you are obviously very good at it, but I'm not sure if that translates to the struggles I'm facing in leading and turning around a business organization."

"Hmmm, interesting. Chase, let me give you a little background on what I've had to do in Philadelphia over the last three years since I took over as head coach. You know that we won the championship this year, but when I first walked into the organization, it was a mess. I needed to set the tone for what the organizational goals were, and share my vision on how we were going to get there. I needed to build a strong and winning team. It was a lot of work, but it was worth it."

Billings continued, "My first task was to evaluate the current situation and develop my game plan for achieving my objective, which was always to build a winning team. I had to understand where I was going, and where I currently was, before I could map out a strategy. Once I developed my strategy, it was as simple as making sure that every day I moved the organization closer to the goal. I don't see your situation as being any different, do you?"

Chase thought about it for a second before responding, "No, I guess the situation is the same in the big picture, and I fully understand the need for developing a strategy, but the problem is I just am not sure how to go about doing it, and then getting everyone to buy in."

"Isn't that what your seminar is for?" asked Coach Billings.

"I thought so, but I'm afraid that if the remaining two days are anything like today, I'll be heading home with no new ideas, and feeling like I wasted an entire week, not to mention the monetary investment," Chase replied. "I really want to lead this company to success, just like you have been able to do with your teams."

The two men didn't say anything to each other for a few moments. They both took drinks from their mugs, and read the words that scrolled across the bottom of the TV screen, several of which were misspelled. When another commercial came on, Coach Billings turned to Chase and said, "Tell you what Chase, I'm here for the rest of the week. I don't do anything while I'm here except sit in here or on the beach. While it might be relaxing, it's not the most enjoyable thing for me. I'd be more than happy to meet with you for the next few days and see if we can come up with a strategy to help you lead your team. What do you say? You up for it?"

"You sure you want to do that?" replied Chase, who was rather surprised at the offer. "This is supposed to be your vacation."

"Chase, I normally work about sixty hours per week. My job doesn't end when the season ends, and it isn't just coaching the team. In essence, I have a multi-million dollar business to run. I'm a workaholic, but I love it, and I love watching my hard work pay off as my team comes together and we achieve each of the goals I've set. I'd be happy to help you out, especially since you aren't coaching any teams that we'd have to play against in the near future," Coach Billings joked.

"Well Coach, I can't pass up an offer like that. Your advice has got to be better than sitting zombie-like through two more days of the seminar. How do you want to do this?"

"Let's grab a table so we can be a little more comfortable. We'll start talking and see what we can accomplish today," Coach suggested as he picked his glass up off the bar and stood up from his stool. "Big Joe, we're just moving over to a table. Can you get us each another drink?"

"You got it coach," Big Joe replied.

Coach Billings led Chase to a table that was in a more secluded area, away from the windows and the table that the three women were using. Chase sat down with his back to the wall, while Billings took the seat directly across from him. This put Billings' back towards the rest of the room, which he purposely did to reduce the chance of being recognized and interrupted by a fan. If one did still happen to stop by, he would be polite, but he had learned a few tricks in order to reduce the chance of that happening when he was having a private meeting. Big Joe arrived with two glasses just as they were getting settled in their chairs.

"Big Joe, you're the best," commented Coach Billings.

The grin on Big Joe's face could not have been wider. "I aim to please," Big Joe replied. "Let me know if you need anything else."

"Ok Chase, tell me about this position of yours, and tell me a little about the company," Billings opened.

Chase explained to Coach Billings that the company was fairly new, having just celebrated its sixth year in business. The business had grown quickly over the first three years, but the last three have seen an increasing decline in sales. Profits have also declined as fixed costs have increased. Needing cash, the company had been recently purchased by a venture capital company, and they wanted to see improvements fast.

The business had been the brain child of a entrepreneur named Shawn Cooper, who had recently been let go by the board of directors. This had been done at the request of the venture capital company, who had lost faith in Mr. Cooper's ability to turn the company around. It seemed to Chase that this move had not gone over well with the employees of the company.

Chase had been recommended for the position by John Zelling, a long-time family friend, who knew one of the key people in the venture capital company. It was through this contact that Chase had gotten an interview and was finally selected to lead the company. This gave Chase an extra incentive to do well, as he didn't want to let down Mr. Zelling.

Chase described the business structure; that he reported to the board of directors, which was made up of people from the capital investment company and other established and successful business executives. Besides Chase, there were currently fifty-two employees working for him. There was a sales department, a small marketing department, a customer service department, a small human resources department, a shipping department, and of course an accounting department. Each department had a director who reported directly to Chase.

Fourteen of the fifty-two employees had been there since the company started, and another thirty had been there for more than four years. Eight of the staff had been there less than a year.

Chase had accepted the job just four weeks ago. He was originally not scheduled to start until the week following the leadership seminar, but the board had asked him to move that up and to start last week. So far, he had only had a chance to meet with each of the department directors and had briefly met with a handful of the employees. The product they delivered was top quality and the market for it was growing. He had reviewed the financial statements and felt that there was major room for improvement, but it would take a lot of hard work from everybody.

Coach Billings had listened intently as Chase explained the company and his current situation. Billings wanted to make sure he had a clear understanding of the situation in his mind, so he asked a few clarifying questions. "Chase, you said that the ousting of the company's leader didn't go over too well. Tell me a little more about that."

Chase thought about it for a few seconds before replying, "I would say that I am basing that on comments made to me by some of the employees, and some comments I overheard. If I were to guess, I think that it is more a fear of change, having new leadership and what that means to their jobs. Some of it I am sure is due to loyalty and personal feelings they had towards the person who had started the company and had hired them in the first place."

"So you would say that the morale isn't too good?"

"I think that it is safe to say that. I haven't witnessed much enthusiasm among the workers."

"OK, so tell me about the directors that report to you. Are they capable?"

"Capable?" Chase hesitated for a few moments as he thought about the question.

Noting Chase's expression, Coach clarified his question. "Can they be the leaders that every team needs? Are they willing to put in the effort? Will they support your decisions and leadership?"

Again Chase took a few moments and considered the coach's question before offering his thoughts. "Honestly Coach, I don't know; it is a little early for me to have developed full opinions of them. I've only just met them and haven't had a chance to really work with them to gather enough information to answer that question. I've met with each of them, and initially they seem ok.

Lisa, who is the Sales Director, has a pretty strong personality, but that might help her in her role. I know that it will be critical to the company's success that I have good directors that will work with me and not against me."

When Chase finished, Coach Billings told him, "Fair enough. Sometimes *I Don't Know* is the hardest thing for a leader to say. Your ability to say that gives me a great deal of hope for you. I want you to also remember that it will take more than good directors-- you'll also need good team members. You know how I mentioned that I thought there would be a lot of parallels between your situation and the one I walked into in Philadelphia?

Let me give you a little background so you can see for yourself. The Philadelphia team had been lead by the same person for seven years prior to me coming aboard. He had been the GM as well as the head coach, so he oversaw the entire organization, just as I do now. The people in the front office, the entire coaching staff as well as most of the team members had been hired under his leadership. When the owner decided it was time to make a change because he didn't like the direction the team was heading, he took action very similar to what your board of directors did.

I then had to step in, knowing that everyone there was concerned in one way or another about the change. I also knew that in order for the organization to get to where I wanted it to be, that I would need people in place that would buy into my vision and direction. I know the steps I took to get there, and I think they may help you lead your team to the level you believe it can be. Do you see the similarities?"

"I do."

"Good to hear. We've got a lot to talk about in the next few days, but that will only be the start for you. You ready to get started?

"I sure am!"

3

Slogan of Purpose

Since Coach Billings and Chase had moved to a table and had been talking, six additional customers had entered the tropical drinking hole. A group of four women and two other gentlemen going stag were now being served refreshing beverages by Big Joe. Since Coach's back was to the other patrons, none of the new vacationers had recognized him. Although the four women were laughing and seemingly enjoying themselves greatly, the Coach and Chase were able to continue their conversation.

"OK, we know what the current situation is, and we'll call that where you are, now, we need to know where you want to be. Do you have a vision of what that might look like?"

"Good question. I know that I want the company to be successful again, but I don't yet have a clear picture in my mind as what that might look like."

"Fair enough Chase, but let me just tell you that knowing where you want to be is as important as knowing where you currently are. You will need to develop a clear picture of what success means, and you are going to need to share that with your organization. Once you and your team share that vision, you'll then be able to ensure that each decision that you make will be one that gets you closer to it. Does that make sense?"

"It sure does."

"If I can offer a suggestion, I would recommend that you meet with the directors within your organization in order to develop that vision. This will help in two ways; first, you will get differing insights and ideas that will be helpful; secondly, you will be able to use this to gauge the level of engagement and competency of your directors."

"I like that idea. I'll make that one of my first priorities when I get back."

"OK, let's take a step back for a second. One of the other key things that you will need to develop is your "RFE", which stands for your Reason For Existence."

"Is that different than your vision?" Chase asked.

"It is very different. Let me try to explain the difference. For our sports team, our RFE is to constantly deliver the most exciting experience for all of our fans. Our vision however, is more specific. It might be something like *To be unanimously considered the most successful sports organization.* Notice that I didn't say a particular sport, but rather to be considered the best in all of sports."

"Now if I tried to give you a non-sports example, let's say you and I worked for a home building company. Our RFE might be something like *We make people's dreams come true.* It's gets to the core essence as to why we are in business in the first place, and more importantly why someone would want to do business with us. Can you see the difference?"

"I think I do. The company's RFE, or Reason For Existence, can be considered our Slogan of Purpose, whereas our company's Vision is how we want to be perceived in the market, by our customers, our competition and ourselves," Chase offered.

"Slogan of Purpose...I like that. You're exactly right. This might be another exercise that you can do with your directors. It might help your marketing team develop some branding materials that line up with your RFE."

"That's another great idea. I can call my directors together to discuss these two items and make sure we are all on the same page. We can then share both our Slogan of Purpose and our Vision with the other team members."

As the two men had been talking, the crowd inside had been steadily increasing. As Chase looked around, he recognized several of the men and women from the leadership seminar audience. Based on the number of people, the day's session must have ended, or else a good number had taken the opportunity during a break to escape and were now looking for comfort in a cold beverage inside a good imitation of an oversized tropical hut. With the increased number of people inside, the sound level had increased to the point where you could no longer hear the consistent rhythm of the reggae music coming from the speakers hidden in the ceiling. Chase became aware that his voice level had increased in order to compete with the higher background noise.

Coach Billings must have noticed as well, as he advised, "How about we head down to the beach to continue talking. It's just going to get more crowded. It always does, and It's getting a little loud in here already." Just as he said it, a loud chant came from a group by the bar. It was the four women who had entered some time ago who had now been joined by three men. Coach was able to get eye contact with Big Joe with the assistance of his waving hand. Big Joe came over to their table within a few minutes.

"Starting to get a little busier I see," Coach said to Big Joe as he approached.

"Just wait until you see this place in a few hours. It will be packed. Everyone wants to come hang out with Big Joe," he said, referring to himself in the third person.

"Big Joe, we're going to head down to the beach for a while. We might be back later, but we should probably close out our tab. Please put everything on my room, and I'll settle up with you later tonight or tomorrow. Is that cool?" Coach asked of his large and seemingly always happy host.

"Not a problem Coach!" Big Joe responded with his ever present smile. Big Joe headed back to see what refills his guests needed at the bar.

Chase and Coach Billings exited the tropical hut. The late afternoon sun was currently blocked by one of several large billowing clouds that were slowly drifting across the sky. Chase was thankful for this, as he still didn't have his sunglasses, and he didn't want to have Coach wait while he ran up and retrieved them.

As they walked through the resort's pathway that led to the beach, Coach asked Chase a question. "Chase, what do you suppose the formula $S = P - E$ stand for."

"Coach, I don't think I've ever heard that one."

"Think about it for a few minutes while we walk to the beach. I want to see what you come up with."

4

S = P - E

In the ten or so minutes that it took the two men to reach the sands of the beach, Chase had been running different words through his mind that would match up with the three letters in the formula Coach had brought up. Coach could see that Chase was struggling to come up with an answer that would fit not only the formula initials, but would also be relevant to their conversation. As they approached an empty bench and sat down facing the water, Coach asked, "Able to come up with anything?"

"No, nothing that makes sense anyways."

"S=P-E is a formula that I learned from a mentor of mine named Jerry. The formula stands for Success equals Performance minus Expectations. In sports, that is easy to correlate. Walking into this last season, the expectations for my team were to make the playoffs. If we hadn't done that, the season would have been perceived as unsuccessful. However, because we were able to go further than was expected, our season was looked at as successful. It would have been successful even if we hadn't won the championship, because our performance was greater than the expectations."

Coach continued, "Chase, the formula works for all things in business. If your sales figures are higher than what was expected, then you would have had a successful campaign. Does this make sense?"

Chase was already ahead of him, thinking of how the formula could be used in judging different aspects of the company's performance. "It does; It makes total sense. Success only happens when your performance is greater than the expectations. I would assume that it would then be extremely important to understand what the expectations are, or else you wouldn't be able to judge if you were indeed successful or not."

"Exactly! However, what I have learned is that this is one area that people really struggle with. Often, expectations are not discussed or documented in the beginning. This is a critical conversation that needs to happen. People will have different understanding of the expectations if the conversation does not happen up front, which will lead to differing levels of perceived success, and could even lead to some people thinking that an endeavor wasn't successful at all," Coach explained.

"I could see how that could happen. Let's say that my

company was launching a marketing campaign. We had decided to use a few different advertising mediums to get our message out there. If we didn't have clear expectations up front, then it would be hard, if not impossible to determine whether each of the mediums were successful or not. We then couldn't use that valuable information in the future when preparing for our next campaign."

"Chase, that is a perfect example. For some reason, one that I cannot explain, we skip over this important conversation on a regular basis. Since Jerry brought it to my attention, I make sure that I do my best to discuss expectations in every aspect of our team's business. This is true especially for people. I make sure that every team member understands what my expectations are of them. It allows me to easily have conversations with them if their performance is not meeting those expectations. Chase, do you do regular performance reviews with your people?"

"I'm not sure what the company has done in the past, but I intend on having reviews completed at least annually for each team member. I can see that making sure each of those team members understands what the expectations are of them would be an important first step."

"Good. We'll talk more about people tomorrow, but coming back to expectations, do you know what is expected of you? Do you know how the Board of Directors will determine if you are successful or not?"

"No, I don't, but I will soon" Chase replied, knowing that this is something that he will need to revisit with the board when he returns.

"You can see why it is so important. Just as you want to make sure that you are judged as being successful based on known variables, your team members will appreciate it as well. It will also assist in your development of company goals, as they will align with what the board will perceive as being successful or not. Now I'll caution you that you might need to temper or manage people's expectations of you and the company. In addition, you'll find that you may need to temper your expectations of others. The expectations need to be reasonable, and not some far-fetched, unattainable or unrealistic goal."

"I understand what you are saying. Take for example my expectations of this leadership seminar. I'm looking at it as unsuccessful, but it may be that my expectations were too high. I was expecting to get all the necessary answers. Perhaps that was unrealistic."

"Great way to look at it. Chase, it almost 5:30 and I need to make some phone calls tonight. How about we call it a day and start back up first thing tomorrow morning?"

"Sounds good to me. I need to call home and check in with the family myself, plus you've given me some things to think about tonight. What time do you want to meet in the morning?"

"Let's say eight am sharp down at Big Joe's. They offer up a decent breakfast and there shouldn't be too many people there in the morning. I've enjoyed our conversation so far, and look forward to continuing it tomorrow," Coach said as he stood up from the bench.

The two men walked back to the resort following the same path they had taken to get to the beach. Their conversation back was more small talk, discussing the resort's amenities and the weather forecast for the next few days. They again wished each other a good evening as Chase exited the elevator as it stopped on his floor.

After entering his room, Chase checked his e-mails using his laptop. He had a dozen e-mails for work. The first one he opened was from his executive assistant, Ellen. She had been sending him an e-mail each day, providing him a summary of any important item that he should be aware of.

Another message was from the director of the customer service department, Kevin. The e-mail was a resignation from one of the customer service personnel, which Kevin had forwarded to Chase. Kevin noted to Chase in the e-mail that this team member had been with the company for a long time, and he expressed his concern that they might risk losing more valued team members over the low morale.

Chase sent a quick reply to Kevin, asking him for his opinion on the person that had tendered their resignation. Was it someone that, if Kevin could have his choice of people on the team, he would select. If so, Chase would be more than happy to reach out to the person and see if he could get them to change their mind and stay.

Chase was happy that Coach Billings had mentioned that they would talk about people the next day, because the company couldn't afford to lose most of its team members. Something had to be done soon to improve morale.

He then read through his other messages.

The last e-mail he opened had come from Fred, the director of the accounting department. It contained the latest sales figures. The information was not surprising to Chase. The downward trend was continuing. Chase wondered to himself how quickly he could get things turned around, even with the advice he was receiving from Coach Billings.

Before shutting down his laptop, Chase typed up and sent an e-mail to his four directors. He wanted to get started on the topics he and coach had discussed today as soon as possible.

Subject: Our Purpose?

Team, I would like each of you to be prepared to discuss your thoughts on our company's purpose for being. (Why are we in business?) Please do not discuss with team members at this point. Will explain more first thing Monday morning.

Thanks,

Chase

Chase called his wife, Reagan, as soon as he had closed his laptop. He couldn't wait to tell her about his conversation with the most famous coach in Philadelphia, and possibly the entire country. He dialed his home number. His wife answered on the third ring. "Hello."

"Hey honey, it's me. How's everything there in Philly?"

"Things are good. No rain today, but it was cloudy. How was the first day? Did you learn anything?"

"The day started off badly, but by the end of the day, it was great. You'll never guess who I met and talked to today." Chase proceeded to tell Reagan about his day, how terrible the sessions were, and how he had met Coach Billings. His voice showed his excitement when he explained how Billings had offered to give him advice on building a winning team, and what they had talked about so far.

"Well, you can't argue with the success he has had, so he most likely knows what he is talking about. So far it sounds like he's given you good advice," Reagan told her husband. Chase could always count on Reagan to tell it to him straight. They had a great relationship, and would bounce ideas and problems off each other on a regular basis. Reagan's parents had named her after their acquaintance, who was the Governor of California at the time. He went on to become their favorite president. Chase thought her name was as unique as she was, but having a name like that made it hard for him to ever find something that had her name already printed on it. She would never receive a keychain or a coffee mug adorned with her name, unless they made a trip to the Reagan Presidential Library some day.

"So, you like these ideas so far? The, what did you call it...Slogan of Purpose, the vision and the success formula, S=P-E. You want to use these in your new position?" Reagan asked.

"I do. They make perfect sense to me, and you can't argue with the success that Coach Billings has had in building high performing teams. I think that if I use some of the techniques he is sharing with me, then I can build a successful team as well. I'm really looking forward to talking with him more tomorrow."

Chase spoke to Reagan for another 20 minutes, listening to how her day went and discussing a proposal they had received from a contractor in regards to having their basement finished.

After hanging up, Chase realized that he had not yet eaten dinner. He contemplated ordering room service, but decided instead to go back down to Big Joe's Oasis. He had noticed that they offered a casual menu featuring sandwiches and burgers, which sounded good to Chase.

Although the sun had set, the air outside was still quite humid and warm. The outside was lit with a wide selection of landscape lights, and many of the palm tree trunks were wrapped with hundreds of lights. All the lighting made the paths leading to the pool very easy to maneuver.

Chase stepped inside the building where he had fortuitously met Coach Billings earlier in the day. There was a good number of men and women sitting at the tables, and this time there was only one vacancy at the bar. Chase sat in the exact same stool he had occupied earlier.

Big Joe was in front of him within a matter of moments, smiling as usual. "Hey my friend, what can I get for you?

"I'm looking to get something to eat. What do you recommend?"

"The burger is fantastic. Best in the world!"

"Sounds good, but now you really have my expectations set high. Hope it's as good as you say Big Joe. And, I'll take an iced tea to drink."

"Coming right up."

Big Joe went to the computer touch screen to enter in the food order. Big Joe then brought Chase's drink to him. "Did your day get any better?"

Chase remembered telling Big Joe about his frustrations with the seminar. "It got a lot better, thanks."

"Yeah, Coach can have that affect on people."

"You know him pretty well?"

"He comes down here every year, but I've known Coach since before that, back from when I used to play. I really liked playing for him, everybody did. He could get more out of you then you ever imagined you could do. He's a straight shooter, and I really respect that."

"I would think it might be hard to push people to perform, but then also gain their respect. How did he do that?"

"You knew exactly what was expected of you, and how

important your performance was to the whole team. If you did a good job, he let you know it, and if you did something wrong, he told you what you did wrong, and what the consequences would be if you kept doing it. He'd explain how it could hurt the team, and how you would be letting others down, as well as letting yourself down. Everything with Coach is about the team. One wins, everyone wins, one fails, everyone fails. You didn't want to be the one that let everyone down, and you didn't want to let Coach down. The thing that was so cool about it, was that we all had fun. It was the greatest time I've ever had."

"That's exactly the type of atmosphere and culture I want to develop at my company. I sure hope I can learn enough from Coach in order to get me headed in that direction."

"You will my friend. He's done great things for me here. He helped me get this place."

"The hotel? You own the hotel?"

Big Joe laughed hard. "No, not the hotel. I own this place." Big Joe tapped his finger on the bar. "Coach helped me get the funding for it several years ago. I lease it from the hotel. He's helped me develop my strategy for making this place successful. I now own two other locations in town, but I like working at this one the best. I use the things that I've learned from Coach to build a good business, where people want to work for me, and where my customers like to come back."

With that comment Big Joe stepped down the bar to help another of his customers. Chase looked around at the people inside the faux tropical retreat and observed the two other workers that were waiting on the tables. They seemed very happy, and their customers seemed to be enjoying the interaction. Chase wondered if this was due to some of Coach's teachings that Big Joe had implemented. He couldn't wait until tomorrow.

Big Joe brought Chase's dinner, which true to Big Joe's claim was one of, if not the best, burger that Chase had ever had. When Chase was finished, Big Joe asked him if it had met his high expectations.

"It sure did. I'll admit I was a little skeptical at the time, but this truly is the best burger I've ever had."

Big Joe leaned in towards Chase and said softly, "S=P-E." He then placed his right palm towards Chase. Chase obliged with a high five, being quite sure that Big Joe had unknowingly helped drive home one of Coach's lessons.

Chase stayed at Big Joe's place for a while after finishing his dinner. The atmosphere was fun, and customers were enjoying themselves. Chase knew that it was that way in big part to what Big Joe has learned from Coach Billings.

As Chase laid in his bed that night, waiting for the vastness of sleep to take over him, he thought again about the main points he and Coach had discussed that day. He decided that he should make some detailed notes before falling asleep, so he climbed out of bed, sat at the desk, and wrote on his note pad.

1. Have a clear understanding of your Reason for Being, or your "Slogan of Purpose."

2. Have a strong vision of how you want the company to be perceived in the market; by your customers, your employees and your competition.

3. Success = Performance minus Expectations (S=P-E): Success is only found when the performance is greater than the expectations. It is critical to discuss and make sure everyone understands what the expectations are. If you don't, then there is no way to measure if you are successful or not.

5

Leadership Philosophy

Chase woke up ten minutes before his alarm went off. He showered, dressed and left his room at 7:45. He went directly to Big Joe's, not wanting to be late. He brought along his portfolio this time, so that he could take notes during their discussions. Chase didn't want to miss or forget a single thing that Coach shared. He also remembered to grab his sunglasses. Chase noticed a good number of people in the elevators and hotel that were carrying their seminar binders, finding their way to the 2nd day's sessions. Chase knew that the knowledge he would gain from Coach Billings would be priceless compared to what those folks were most likely in for.

Chase entered Big Joe's, and found Coach sitting at the same table they had occupied the day earlier.

"Good morning Coach," Chase offered as he moved around the table to where Billings could see him. Coach stood up and offered his hand once again in the traditional American greeting.

"Good morning Chase. Did you sleep well last night?"

"I did, thanks. How about yourself?"

"I sleep like a baby every night," Coach revealed.

"Even before a big game?" Chase asked.

"Yep. I've never had a problem sleeping, because I know that every day I did everything I could to make sure my team was prepared for battle. In your case, you'll be battling with your competition, not on the playing field, but in the marketplace. Let's get some breakfast, and then we can start talking about your team."

"If breakfast tastes as good as their burgers, I'm ready."

"Ah, you came back here for dinner last night?"

"I did, and had a good talk with Big Joe. He's pretty amazing. Runs a very nice business here."

The hostess came by the table and took their breakfast order. She was very pleasant and helpful, just as Chase would have expected from one of Big Joe's employees.

"Ok Chase, I'm going to share with you some of my thoughts on team members. They may be somewhat radical to what you've heard in the past or what you've seen out there in the business world, but I can assure you that they work. You can't have a great organization if you don't have great people. You ready to have an open mind and talk about what it takes to get there?"

Chase was very curious and anxious to hear what Coach had to say. "You bet I am."

"Let me tell you a little about how I approach a team when I first walk in. This should be relevant to your situation, but would also work if you've been there a while and need to improve the overall situation. First are the expectations."

"We talked about the importance of those yesterday, and I completely agree."

"Well Chase, this is a little different. We're still talking about expectations, but now we're talking about what your team can expect from you, and what you will expect from them as a group."

"I'm not sure I follow you."

"This is your opportunity to share with your entire team your leadership philosophy. Here's an example to help you understand what I mean; When I walked into my first staff meeting, I presented each of the team members a document that laid out my approach to leadership, what they can expect from me, and what I will expect from them in return. I also gave them a clear heads-up on what my pet peeves are, so there wouldn't be any surprises."

"A few of the phrases I know from heart, because I keep this document hanging in my office to constantly keep me on track.

- I will give 100% towards the success of this team. I expect each of you to do the same.
- We are all human, and we will make mistakes. I vow to learn from each of mine, and I expect you to do the same.
- There will be times when I need to make tough decisions, which will impact some or all of you. When I do, I will try my best to make sure you understand my reasoning.
- I will be honest with you in all matters. In exchange, when I ask you for your input, I expect you to be honest with me.
- I will represent this organization in a professional manner. I expect each of you to do the same.
- I will be on time to every meeting. I expect each of you to do the same.

That is a few of them from my list. What you need to do Chase, is to develop your own list, and share it with your team. This is not something that most leaders do, but I promise you it will make a difference."

Chase had been busily writing down Coach's examples as he was reciting them off the top of his head. "I'll tell you Coach, I think it's a great idea. I've never heard of anything like it, but I can see how it would help. I know that if someone shared this with me, I'd appreciate it."

"Glad to hear that you buy into it Chase. Now, just like you said that you have never heard of anything like it, it will be new to your team members. Make sure you walk them through it so that they understand that this is coming from you, and that you believe in every single item that you list, OK?"

"I agree Coach"

"Chase, I'll have my list sent to you through e-mail. You can use any portion of it that you want, but you should make up a few of your own. Take ownership of it, because it needs to be true to you."

"That would be great Coach. I can personalize it, and I will own it."

"Good, now let's talk about setting the stage for the right kind of culture."

6

Demand Professionalism

"Chase, you will need to plant the seeds for the proper culture, and it will take ongoing nurturing, which comes from you doing the proverbial *Walking the Walk*. You need to demand professionalism, and settle for nothing less."

"You're talking about how they interact with our customers?"

"Not just that, although that is a big part of it. I'm talking about every aspect of the business. It might make sense for us to make a list of items, since you have a pad of paper there in front of you. I'll give you a few to start off, and then we'll build the list together.

1. *Voice mail messages, both the ones your employees leave and the ones that your customers hear when they call*

2. *The way the phone is answered*

3. Making sure that everything that goes out has correct spelling and grammar

"You starting to get the idea?"

"Yes, I see where you are going with this. Let me add a few more."

4. The way we are dressed

5. The way our building looks, both on the outside and the inside

"Those are good ones Chase. I think you understand the point I'm trying to make. In essence, every single thing that could possibly be seen or heard by anyone, whether they are a customer or not, needs to be done in a professional way. This goes for your website, your company vehicles, your people, your advertising, everything. On my teams, I demand professionalism. For the athletes, as well as everyone else involved. Remember what I said earlier, it's about the entire team. Nothing can disrupt a well functioning team more than a person who acts in an unprofessional manner, and I have no problem releasing that person from the team, no matter who they are or what position they have within the company."

"Coach, I've seen this first hand on two separate occasions. I worked for one company where one of the sales reps was openly fabricating information in order to get sales. Because he was bringing in a ton of revenue, management turned a blind eye. It came back to bite them when customers started realizing that the promises he made were not true. They stopped doing business with that rep, and with the company. The entire company suffered because they allowed this level of unprofessionalism continue.

In the other situation, a particular franchisee who had been in the system for a very long time, was allowed to use profane and threatening language, both verbally and in e-mails. It was not a very pleasant environment to work in. When others, including myself, complained to upper management, we were told, "*Oh, that's just Richard. We know he's a hot-head, but he's been in the system for a very long time and he knows a lot about this business. Just try to ignore him.*" Even worse, they gave him additional responsibilities because he would make a big stink about something and they would cave in just to keep him appeased. Well, we lost a lot of good people because they didn't want to work in that type of environment, and he was such a distraction, that our productivity suffered as well. Unfortunately, the company didn't do anything about him until they got sued. It ended up costing them a lot of money and drove them to near bankruptcy. If they would have demanded professionalism, like you suggest, then things could have been much different and they could still be a market leader. What was sad about the whole situation, is that Richard thought that he was respected. He was a great reminder that respect is earned, and not something that you can try to demand or intimidate out of someone."

"Great examples Chase, and I could give you quite a few more from the sports world where one athlete acts in an unprofessional manner, and it affects the entire organization. At minimum it is an unwanted distraction. At worst, it can tear teams apart. Now, the tone will be set by you. You will need to demand professionalism, and settle for nothing less. If you let one thing slide, you will lose all credibility. Once you lose your credibility, or the respect of others, it will be next to impossible to get back. You'll need to demand professionalism both from others, and from yourself. Make sense?"

"It makes perfect sense." Chase had to switch to a new, clean page as he continued taking notes.

Their breakfast arrived, and as soon as Chase took his first bite, he knew that Big Joe must have taken Coach's advice. Everything was prepared perfectly, and the staff was both friendly and extremely professional. Big Joe demanded professionalism. Chase could tell.

"Chase, what I'd like for you to do is put together your Professionalism Manifesto. You'll start by making a listing of every potential public touch-point with your company. It will include the items we already discussed, like phone answering, your building, you company vehicles, etc.   You will document the expected level of professionalism for each of these touch-points. You'll then share with your entire team the importance of every aspect being done in the most professional manner. You team members will respond well to this, as everyone wants to work for a professional organization.   You'll deal with the usual pushback to change, but as long as you communicate the reason behind it, they will more easily understand and accept it. We'll talk more about leading through change tomorrow."

"That would be good, because I know that changes in a company can sometimes be tough for people to accept."

"Let's finish up our breakfast, and then we'll start back up again. That way you'll have room on the table to take notes."

During the rest of their breakfast meal, the two exchanged casual conversation on subjects such as their families, hobbies and their favorite movies and books. Chases told Coach about his wife, Reagan, how they had met, how he had proposed, and what their goals were in life. During the conversation, they were surprised to discover that they both shard the same favorite author, *Dean Koontz*.

7

Developing Strengths

With their delicious breakfast completed, and the table promptly cleared by one of Big Joe's staff, Coach Billings brought up the next subject he wanted to discuss with Chase.

"Chase, tell me your thoughts and approach to developing your people."

Chase thought about the question for a few moments before answering. "I think personal development is very important. In the past, I've talked with each person that reported to me. I evaluate them in regards to the different competencies required for the position, and then I develop a unique development plan for each of them to address their weaknesses."

"And tell me how that has worked for you."

"Well, I've had some successes, but I've also had a good number of people that never really overcame those weaknesses."

"Chase, you are like most managers. You focus on their weaknesses and not their strengths, or their natural abilities. I believe that when you do this, you are missing a big opportunity. Let me try and give you an example or two from the sports world and see if it might make sense. Imagine you had a quarterback on your football team that couldn't throw the ball deep, however, he was very accurate with his short and medium range passes. Now, should you focus your efforts on getting him to throw the deep pass better, or would you figure out a way to utilize his strength to help you move the ball down the field? Or, if you like baseball better, imagine you have a team member that could hit the ball and catch extremely well, but couldn't run that fast. Would you make him work on his running speed, or would you put him in a position that would be better suited for his strengths?"

Chase pondered the scenarios for a few moments before offering his thoughts. "In both situations, it seems like it would be better for the individual, and for the overall team, if I focused on their strengths instead of their weaknesses. But doesn't it make sense to do both?"

"Sure, I'm not saying to ignore someone's weakness, especially if it is a core competency needed to do the job. What I'm saying is that you will have much better success if you focus the majority of your time helping a person leverage their strengths or natural abilities in a position rather than their weaknesses. Going back to those two scenarios, if you were to take that quarterback, and work with him to understand the offense so that he can read a situation and throw an accurate short or medium pass, wouldn't that person, and for that matter the entire team, gain more than if I wanted him to spend most of his time working on his arm strength? Think back to the San Francisco 49ers when Joe Montana was their quarterback. He didn't have the strongest arm, but he was very good at the short and medium length passes. His coach understood this, helped him work on it, and designed a system to take advantage of those strengths."

"Ok, so if I bring that example into my world, if I had a sales person that was very good talking to people in person, but was not very good on the phone, I would be better off helping him leverage his natural ability of talking one-on-one with potential clients, instead of making him spend a good amount of time improving his phone cold-calling skills. Is that a fair example?"

"Yes, and let me add that there have been numerous times where I have moved a person to a different position because their strengths better aligned with it rather than their old position. Chase, there may be times where you will need to do the same.

You'll need to explain why you believe the move would be beneficial for the person and the company, but when you are right about it, the person will be very thankful, more satisfied, and as a result they will be more productive. You'll find a good number of All-Stars that at one point in their career were moved from one position to another to take advantage of their strengths."

"I could see where you would get results in a shorter amount of time if you focused on leveraging their strengths, rather than spending a large amount of time on overcoming their weaknesses."

"Oh, you definitely will. Just remember not to forget completely about their weaknesses. The goal is to help them leverage their strengths to be successful, which will lead to the team being successful. What you will want to do is to develop a Growth Plan for each of your team members, focusing on leveraging their natural abilities and strengths, with a lesser focus on their weaknesses. I would put this responsibility on your directors and your HR department, after you explain to them the reasoning behind it."

"Coach, this is great stuff. I wonder why this isn't part of the management mainstream. It makes so much sense to me."

"I don't know Chase. The sports world has been doing it for decades. Somehow the business world hasn't caught on."

Chase was busily taking notes, so Coach sat back and waited for him to finish before moving on to his next topic.

Section 2

Winning Teams

Don't Just

Happen

8

Leveraging Free Agency

"Chase, there is another key tool that allows sports teams to build the best team possible, but for some reason the business world has never utilized. It's called Free Agency. I'm sure you've heard of it."

"Sure Coach, but I'm not sure how we would use it."

"Let me try and explain what I mean. My job is to put together a team with the best possible people in each position, whether they are on the field or in the front office. Each person on my team knows that if they aren't performing at the level I need, and there is someone else out there that I could bring in to replace them, then I have a duty to the overall team to do so. It is part of our culture, but for some reason, in the business world, leaders allow people who are not performing at the top level to stay around for years, while others are out there that could come in and perform at a much higher level. This is a throwback to our parent's generation, when a person stayed at the same company for their entire life. There was a strong level of loyalty on both sides. Those days have been long gone, but business hasn't changed. I can tell you that if you don't have a Winning Team culture, then the majority of your people are already playing the free agency game, and they will move to another company if an opportunity comes along that they feel will be beneficial for them. Why is it Chase that businesses can't, or maybe for a better term, *won't* do the same? Instead, they settle for mediocre performers"

"Wow Coach, that is a very interesting argument! I know that normally we don't start looking for people unless someone gives notice, or if we've recently let somebody go."

"Exactly, and what impact does that have on your business? Having an open position, with nobody to step in, would be devastating to my team. I'm sure that it hurts your business as well."

"Absolutely. Others have to pick up the slack in the meantime, so everyone's productivity suffers."

"Now, imagine if you had the same type of culture in your business as we do in sports. Everyone knows that the goal of the company is to be as successful as possible, and that means that you want and need the best possible people in each position. Do you think that people would put in their best effort in that type of culture?"

"They surely would, but isn't there a fine balance needed? I mean, you don't want people to be scared for their jobs all the time, right?"

"Chase, you continue to impress me. You are exactly right, there is a balance. It is the overall culture you develop that makes that balance work. On one side, you're people need to know and understand that they are expected to perform at the highest level, or they run the risk of you bringing in someone else who will. On the other side, you create a winning environment, where people enjoy what they are doing. When they are happy with the environment, then it's easier for them to do a better job, which reduces the risk of you needing to make changes very often."

"I'm not sure how my HR person will react to such an approach. It seems that there is a hesitancy to cut people from the team, even underperformers, without having a long paper trail."

"I understand. You'll need to talk to them, explain why you believe this strategy makes sense, and work together with them to execute it properly. If you do this right, there won't be a single person that can say they didn't understand what was expected of them. In the long run, your turnover will go down. The fact is that unless you have a contract with someone, then you have the right, and I would say obligation, to fill each position with the best person. Most likely, the majority of people in their current position will stay, and with you explaining exactly what the expectations are of them, their productivity will increase. In sports, we hold drafts, we trade players, and we sign free agents. While you can't trade players to your competition, you can and should always be looking to bring on new and better talent. You may sometimes need to bring on a person even if you don't have a opening, if you feel they have the talent level that you are looking for. You'll save money in the long run, even if you have to carry an extra salary or two once in a while, because your turnover will go down and your productivity will increase."

"That's a lot to consider. It makes sense, it is just such a drastically different approach. Do you know if others have tried this?"

"I do. They had the same initial reservations and concerns that you have. It didn't take them long though, to see the benefits of the approach. Chase, there is nothing that says you need to settle for someone, just because they have been in that position for a while. You'll find that most people want to work around people that are productive and are winners. You start improving the quality of people that work for you, and everyone's attitude, productivity and results will improve. Those that complain, are most likely ones that are not performing at the level you need them to. What I'd like for you to do is think about this tonight, right down some ideas on how you could implement this approach into your culture, and we'll revisit it again before we finish up this week."

While Chase finished taking notes on this topic, Coach ordered each of them cups of coffee. It was, as everything else in Big Joe's, one of the best tasting cups of coffee around.

9

It's a Team Sport

Coach took a long sip of his coffee, then set his cup down. "Chase, if I was to tell you that in order for your business to be extremely successful, you need to take a page from my profession and build a true team environment, what would you say?"

Chase followed suit and put his coffee cup down in front of him. "I guess I would say that a true team environment would mean that every single person within the organization, no matter what their position is, needs to be working towards the same goal."

"Good start. Now, have you ever been a part of a team where one person isn't pulling their weight?"

"Absolutely."

"How did you feel about that?"

"Everybody else on the team was mad, at both the person and at management for not dealing with it right away."

"That is a typical experience. Unfortunately, this exact

experience you described is all too common. I can give you a long list of examples where a very talented and capable athlete, for a variety of reasons, became a huge distraction for the team. It is something that should not be tolerated. Many of them become big news stories, while others didn't.

I'm also aware of dozens of stories in the business world where a team member becomes a distraction. It's incumbent on the manager or leader to address the situation right away. The team member needs to be made aware of the impact their behavior is having on the team, exactly what changes in behavior is expected, and what the consequences are if they don't change.

The trouble really starts when management, whether it's a coach in my world, or a manager in the business world, allows the behavior to continue because they would rather avoid the situation, or they incorrectly feel that the person is too important to the overall team. You told me about two situations yesterday that you witnessed personally. I could tell that these really affected you."

"You're right, they did. But, I've also seen situations where someone is having ongoing personal problems that are impacting their work. How do you suggest these types of situations get handled?"

"First, let me say that I am not advocating you or anyone else turning into some axe man who is just looking to fire people. What I am saying though, is that you need to build a winning team. If someone has a personal situation that is impacting their work, then we as leaders have a responsibility to address it with them so that they understand what impact their choice of actions is having on the overall team. You can and should have empathy for their situation, but you should also hold them accountable for their choice of actions. Chase, let me get on my soapbox for a minute here. Anyone you hire will be of an adult age, correct?"

"Yes."

"Ok, as an adult, we make hundreds of choices every day, not just what we are going to wear, or what we are going to eat, but how we react in situations we find ourselves in. If I have a problem at home, I still have the ability to make choices about how I am going to handle a situation at work. When you run into a situation where a team member is having difficulty at work due to an outside issue, then you, or one of your leaders within the company, needs to sit down with that person right away. First, make sure that they understand that you support them and will help in any way the company can. This is just being a good human being. Secondly, you need to make sure they are aware of the impact their choice of actions is, or could have on the overall team. You also need to ensure that the team member understands that those types of choices cannot be allowed to continue, and what consequences there would be if it does continue."

"I like how you call them choice of actions. As I hear you talking it through, I understand what you are saying. Although we have some tough situation, whether it be outside of work or an internal situation, we, as adults, have the ability to choose how we are going to act, or react in a particular situation at work. Is that an accurate paraphrase?"

"That's it exactly. What I see happen too often, is that the leader allows the choice of action, or the behavior, to continue because they feel sorry for the person. You're really not helping the person when you do that, and you definitely aren't being a leader for your team.

Chase, I've had this situation so many times in my professional life, with team members going through divorces, child custody battles, family illnesses, you name it. As soon as I become aware of behavior that is out of the norm, or is just simply unacceptable, I will sit down with that person and talk. I need to find out what is driving the behavior. If it is a personal situation, then I will take every step I can to help that person get through it. They know immediately that if they are willing to make the proper choices to correct the behavior, then I, along with the team or company will stand behind them with whatever creative resources are needed.

I'm telling you from experience that doing this brings so much back to the company in the long run, but it is also just the right thing to do. Now, I will also let the team member know that I have a responsibility to the rest of the team also, and that their choice of action is not acceptable and if it continues I will be required to remove them from the team environment. Depending on the situation, this may be vacation, unpaid leave, or quite frankly, a dismissal. Fortunately, I've only had to take this action a few times, but I don't regret it, because it was the right thing to do for the rest of the team. Chase, everyone wants to be a part of a good, winning team. But, I will tell you that you will never find one that does not have at least one strong leader, whether it be a coach, a player, a manager, a director, whatever."

"Coach, in my experiences, the rest of the team will also be supportive of the person's situation, but they will also look to management to correct any behavior that is disrupting the team."

"You are right Chase, and if management doesn't take the appropriate action to make sure the choice of actions changes for the better, in a expeditious fashion, then the team will lose confidence in them quickly."

"I've seen that happen Coach. I want to make sure that it doesn't happen under my watch."

"Chase, I've seen people do incredible things while dealing with the most dramatic and heartbreaking personal issues. I've seen athletes have record performing days right after the death of a parent. I've seen a person on my ticket sales staff have an incredibly positive attitude at work after learning of her child's serious illness. These people chose to not allow their personal situations negatively affect their performance, and thus didn't hurt their teams. I make sure that I recognize and reward this type of choice of action, for they are a positive example for the entire team. Again, it comes down to the choices a person makes. Chase, you are going to have bad days, and you, like all of us, are going to have challenges in your personal life that you will need to deal with. While you are dealing with those things, you still have the power to choose how you will deal with other people, and whether we react with a positive attitude or a negative one. You as a leader need to foster, and require, that your team members make a positive choice of action, again, leading them by example. "

"Coach, I'm sure you know this, but this approach just makes so much sense to me. It is like the haze is lifted and I can see clearly. What surprises me the most, is that these are practical, common sense approaches, but most companies that I know of don't utilize them."

"You are right Chase. To set the right expectations, I will tell you that it will take a while for you to develop this level of a team culture, but once it takes hold, you will see amazing results; team members will be helping each other; productivity will sky-rocket; turnover will decrease dramatically; job satisfaction will improve, for you and everyone else. Perhaps most importantly, sales and profits will improve."

"It won't happen at all if I don't start somewhere, and the principles you have shared so far are great tools to help me. Do you have any more suggestions when it comes to developing a winning team?

"I sure do, but let's take a quick break and let you catch up on your notes."

Chase busily wrote notes for the next few minutes. He wished he had brought a digital recorder with him.

10

Attitudes are Contagious

"Chase, I want to talk about the importance of attitudes. I've seen guys with a high level of god-given talent fail because they had poor attitudes. On the flip side, I've witnessed people with average talent succeed because they had a positive attitude. I expect that you have witnessed the same."

Chase's mind quickly scanned his memories for people that fit each of these descriptions. "I sure have."

"Besides a yawn, an attitude is one of the most contagious things you will ever encounter. What you want is for positive attitudes to spread throughout your team, and to make sure that negative ones do not have a chance to catch on and spread."

Chase couldn't help but chuckle. "Coach, it's incredible how you can take these different and complex subjects, and break them down into straight forward, common sense pieces. I've witnessed the effect negative attitudes can have on a team so many times, I can't tell you. I need to make sure that this doesn't happen within my team. If I was to take a guess, I would say that what I need to foster in my entire organization, starting with myself, is a Winning Attitude."

Coach Billings smiled. "Chase, I'm glad you are not going to be the coach of one of my competitors." The two men laughed.

"Seriously though, scientists aren't able to quantify the power of a winning attitude. It isn't something that is measurable, but it is one of the most powerful things I have ever witnessed. It can make the difference between winning or losing, both in sports and in business. It also isn't something that can be demanded by leadership, or put in place with a memo. It, like the team culture, takes effort on the part of leadership to develop. It will start with you, and it will be your responsibility to make sure that the only contagious attitude in your organization is a Winning Attitude. Do you have any thoughts on how you might go about doing this with your new team? "

"Wow, that's a pretty deep question. Just off the top of my head, one thing I think I would do is to share with the team true and inspirational stories where having a winning attitude helped either an individual or an organization achieve success."

"That would definitely help get things started. I can

probably send you a few examples of this, as I have used a similar approach in the past. What else do you think might help?"

"Man Coach, you're really putting me on the spot on this one." Chase paused for a few moments while he collected his thoughts. "Ok, I've got some other ideas that would help us create and foster a winning attitude.

1. Create a small task force that is made up of people that already show the ability to keep a winning attitude. Have them develop ideas and plans that we could implement across the entire company.
2. Put together a rewards or recognition program for those people that exhibit the behavior that we are looking for.
3. Develop posters and other motivational materials that we can use to keep the message out there on a regular basis.

I think these things could really help us develop a Winning Attitude."

"Those are four really good ideas. You might want to write those down on your notepad before we move on to another topic. By the way, on the motivational posters, I have a good collection of quotes that I have used. You might be able to leverage some of them into the posters, or whatever type of materials you develop. I'll make sure I send those to you along with the true-life examples by e-mail later this week."

"That would be great Coach. I know I've mentioned it already, but I can't tell you how much I appreciate you spending time with me and sharing your thoughts and ideas."

Chase got busy updating his notes. Coach got them each a glass of iced tea.

11

Have Fun

Coach began again when he saw that Chase was done writing. "There's one last topic that I want to discuss in regards to people. Here's a question for you Chase, why do you think people leave a job for another one?"

"Well, I've heard it said that people don't quit a company, they quit a manager. I think that might be true in a lot of cases, but I also think that people leave a company for a few reasons as well; first, they may not like the overall culture; second, they may be offered better benefits or pay at another company; and third, they may just be bored in their current role or position and are looking for something more exciting."

"In my experience Chase, you are exactly right. Those are all key reasons that a valued team member might give you for leaving your organization. Moving to another job is a scary thing for most people. There may be a promise of better pay, but there are also great unknowns, such as the culture, and the people they will be working for and with. People aren't normally looking for another position unless they are unhappy with their current one, and the pain of moving becomes less than the pain of staying where they are. The sad thing, or, depending on how you look at it, the good thing is that you have a great deal of control over each of these things. Let's take them one at a time. You mentioned that they may leave because they don't like the overall culture of the company. Well, culture starts at the top, and that's you. We've already discussed some great ways for you to change the culture to that of a winning team, and that people want to be associated with winning teams. That will help you keep the valued team members that you want to have on your team."

"I agree Coach, I think that the implementation of some of the things we have discussed is going to go a long way in making the culture one that everyone will enjoy and prosper in."

"Chase, I believe that the next one you mentioned was that they can get better benefits or pay from another company. To this one, I would tell you that money isn't everything, so this one is really tied to some other reason, such as job satisfaction. Chase, I've seen some athletes turn down large salary raises to stay on my teams. When I discuss it with them, they tell me that they are really happy to be part of the team, and that they wouldn't want to play anywhere else. That's how you want your valued team members to feel about your company. You need to pay a fair wage, but building a Winning Team culture will allow you to keep and attract top talent without having to pay overinflated salaries, because they will really enjoy working for you.

"That makes a lot of sense to me Coach," Chase said as he was again busily taking notes on Coach's valuable input.

"Now the third item you mentioned is also tied to job satisfaction. If someone gets bored, or as I believe you put it, looking for something more exciting, then I will tell you that this is a situation where leadership has failed. It's pretty hard to get bored when you are part of a Winning Team. The energy in the organization will continue to build upon itself naturally, as long as the leadership allows the team to enjoy it and have fun. Let's talk through a few situations and you can give me your thoughts on each of them."

"Think back to yesterday morning when you were in the seminar. You were bored because you didn't feel like you were learning anything new, but it was also because you weren't enjoying yourself. Would you have been more engaged if you felt like you were having fun?"

"Sure, that would have made a huge difference. I would have stayed the rest of the day if I found it meaningful or informative."

"Ok, good. Now, we've all been to parties or get-togethers, either in a professional setting or a personal one. I've been to ones that are fun and enjoyable, and I've been to ones where you feel that you are at a funeral. You know what I mean about the latter?"

"Oh yes, I've been to those before. I couldn't wait to get out, and would look for any reason to leave."

"In which one did the time go by the fastest?"

"That's easy Coach, at the ones where you are having fun, the time seems to fly by, where it seems to crawl along when you are at one that is painfully boring or not enjoyable."

"Good, now at which one did you feel that your time was better spent, and was more fulfilling?"

"Again, easy question. The parties where you enjoy yourself are much more fulfilling. You never feel like you wasted your time when you enjoyed yourself."

"Ok Chase, one last scenario. I see that Big Joe walked in a few moments ago. It seems to me that each one of Big Joe's team members here enjoy themselves, and that Big Joe has successfully created a Winning Team environment, would you agree?"

"Absolutely, you can tell that everyone that works here enjoys their job."

"And what impact does that have on you as a customer, Chase?

"It makes my interaction with them and Big Joe's establishment more enjoyable. I think that even if I walked in here having a bad day, which I was yesterday, that it would be impossible to stay in a sour mood with all the positive energy that they have here. Before you even ask, Coach, I can see how that would be true for the team members as well. It would be impossible to have a bad day at work if you were immersed in nothing but positive and fun vibes."

"That is the importance of having fun. The same rules apply to work as they do to the seminar or the parties we just discussed."

"Again, I absolutely agree with you on this one Coach."

"I've heard the saying so many times, *If you're doing what you love, then you never have to work a day in your life.* I'm sure you've heard it too?"

"Sure, I've heard that too."

"Chase, In my opinion, it's a load of bull. I don't care what you are doing, there are going to be situations and days that are stressful. There are going to be days where you will want to pull your hair out. There will be days when you are completely worn out, both mentally and physically. It's a part of business. Take me; I love what I do for a living, but I can tell you that there are many days when I work my butt off. I'm not complaining, just stating a fact. Work is work, but it doesn't have to be boring, tedious or terrible. Life on this earth is too short, and we spend a large percentage of our time here at work. Having fun is important to our health, and I'm sure you won't be surprised to hear that when people have fun, they are more productive. When a person has fun at work, they have a less chance of leaving to go work somewhere else. Chase, when your people are having fun at work, it's much easier to have a winning team. Does that make sense to you?"

"It does. I think I can come up with some ideas on how to

infuse some fun into the work environment, while obviously still maintaining a professional and Winning Team culture."

"Chase, I think you will come up with some great ideas, and I can't wait to hear about them. We've talked about some important aspects of building a winning team this morning, especially in regards to your people. I propose that since it is already past one o'clock, we get some lunch, and then break for the day. I'd like for you to work on some of the topics we discussed, and we can meet back up tomorrow morning to go over them, and then discuss some additional topics related to strategy and execution. How does that sound?"

"I think that's a great idea. I can't wait to start putting some ideas together on all the things we talked about today, and I can't believe it's already lunch time. Like you said, time goes by much faster when you are enjoying yourself, and I definitely am enjoying these discussions with you."

Chase and Coach each ordered a sandwich for lunch. The waitress that took their order had, as Chase had expected, a pleasant and bubbly personality. Big Joe was behind the bar engaged in conversations with several of his patrons. Chase watched him for a few moments. Big Joe's smile was larger than life, and each of the customers were laughing along with him. Big Joe, along with his team members, thoroughly enjoyed their jobs, and each customer enjoyed dealing with them. This is what Chase needed at his company, and he couldn't wait to start moving it in that direction.

When Chase and Coach finished eating their meals, they agreed to meet back at Big Joe's the next morning at 8:oo once again. After charging the meals to his room, Chase excused himself and headed upstairs to start putting some ideas down on paper. He wanted to make sure that Coach was impressed with the things he had come up with, but he also wanted to develop strong ideas that he could start implementing as soon as he got back that next week.

12

Chase's Homework

When Chase entered his room, he opened the curtains that concealed the glass sliding door out to his balcony. He slid open the heavy glass door, allowing the sights, smell and sound of the ocean to flood his senses. He sat at the large desk, and looked over the notes he had taken during his morning session with Coach Billings. He had several pages of notes. Because he had hurriedly written each key point down during the conversation, he took the time to read through each page. Chase then rewrote the key points down on clean pages, making sure that he captured every to-do task that Coach had discussed.

Leadership Philosophy

- Need to share with entire team
  - Written document, provided to each team member
  - Post copy in my office as a reminder
- ❖ TO DO: Develop my Leadership Philosophy

Demand Professionalism

- Do not allow unprofessional behavior
  - Can disrupt the entire organization
- Tone is set with me. I must "Walk the Walk"
- ❖ TO DO: Develop Professionalism Manifesto
  - List every potential public touch-point
  - Document expectations for each one
  - Share with entire team

Developing Strengths

- Leverage each team member's strengths / natural abilities
- Will see quicker results / higher productivity
- ❖ TO DO: Share with Directors
  - Have directors develop growth plan for each team member
    - Focus on strengths / natural abilities

Leverage Free Agency

- Utilize Winning Culture like sports teams

- Don't settle for mediocre team members

- Will reduce turnover in long run, increase productivity

❖ TO DO: Develop ideas for incorporating into our culture

Team Sport

- Person not pulling their own weight
    - Has negative impact on team / productivity
    - Need to address situation immediately
- Choice of Actions
    - Address any behavior that is out of norm / unacceptable

- ♦ If personal issue, help them in any way company can
- ♦ Focus on their "Choice of Action" and impact on team
- ♦ Explain consequences if behavior persists
- ▪ Reward proper Choice of Actions
- ❖ TO DO: Develop Reward / Recognition program

Attitudes are Contagious

- ▪ Need to foster Winning Attitudes
  - ♦ Extremely powerful
  - ♦ Can make difference between winning and losing
  - ♦ Takes effort on part of leadership to develop
  - ♦ Starts with me

- Create and Maintain Winning Attitude
  - Create Task Force
  - Utilize Rewards / Recognition Program
  - Develop motivational materials
- ❖ TO DOs:
  - Review Coach's e-mails
  - Share plan with Directors
  - Create Task Force

Have Fun

- Why people leave a job
  - Unhappy with culture
  - Environment not fun
  - Position is not challenging
- When environment is fun...
  - People enjoy themselves

- Day passes faster

- Higher level of fulfillment / satisfaction

- Lower turnover rates

- Higher productivity

❖ TO DO: Develop ideas for incorporating fun into environment / culture

Chase spent the next few hours working on each of his to-do items. When he was done, he reviewed each of the points. He was happy with the list, but also realized how much work needed to be done. He didn't mind one bit, since he was so excited about each of the topics, and the positive impact he felt each of them would have on the organization. He was feeling much more confident in his ability to create a Winning Team, and couldn't wait to get started. He checked his e-mail to make sure there were not any critical issues that he needed to address. He again had about a dozen messages, including the daily recap from Ellen. Kevin had responded to his e-mail about the employee that had tendered their resignation. Chase was happy to read that Kevin felt that the person wouldn't be among his choice of employees, and that he didn't feel it necessary for Chase to reach out to the person. Chase then worked on several of his to-dos for the next few hours.

Chase's cell phone rang. He looked at the clock on his nightstand as he reached for his phone. It was a few minutes after five. The cell phone's display showed that it was Reagan calling. Chase answered. "Hello."

"Hey there, I'm just on my way home. I was anxious to hear about your day with Coach Billings. How did it go?"

"It was incredible. I hope someday you can meet him. He has this incredible perception about leadership and building winning teams. It's no wonder that he has had such great success in his profession."

"What did you guys talk about today?"

"We talked a lot about people; their attitudes, teamwork, and having fun. He gave me some great ideas on how to start building and then maintaining a winning team."

"I wish the leadership in my company would learn a thing or two about that. It sure hasn't been much fun there lately. Tell me more about his ideas."

Chase went into more detail about the different topics he and Coach Billings had discussed, and shared with Reagan some of the ideas he had come up with that he was going to share with Coach the next day. Reagan gave him some additional ideas, which he incorporated into his notes.

They then discussed Reagan's day and her plans for the evening. They chatted for another thirty minutes before saying goodbye. Chase ate dinner at Big Joe's once again that evening. There were several people there that Chase recognized from the leadership seminar, including the one gentleman that Chase had shared the elevator with the previous afternoon. Chase approached him.

"How is the seminar going? Has it gotten any better?"

"No, not really. What happened to you? You didn't attend today's session?"

"No, I was doing some private work."

"Well, one thing's for sure, you didn't miss much. Sometimes these things are good, and sometimes they aren't.

Tomorrow afternoon is the keynote speaker. I've never heard of him, but hopefully he will be good. That's quite a bummer that you wasted your time coming down here, and didn't get anything out of it."

"Actually, it hasn't been a total waste. I think this week was exactly what I needed. I need to get some dinner. Have a good evening."

"You too."

Chase didn't disclose to the man that he had been schooled in leadership over the last two days by one of the top coaches in the country. He didn't mention it not out of deceit, but rather he didn't want to betray Coach's confidence. He felt comfortable telling Reagan all about it, but without knowing whether Coach would be ok with him saying something to others, he would keep it to himself.

After a delicious dinner, Chase took a stroll over to the beach area. The tide was at its peak. The near-full moon illuminated the foaming water being pushed up the beach by each crashing wave. Each time it would get close to the bench where Chase sat before retreating back, preparing for another push.

The sounds of the crashing waves was very calming. Chase sat there for a little over thirty minutes, thinking once again about the lessons he had received from Coach, formulating plans to incorporate each of them into his approach and the company's culture. He then returned to his room to incorporate his newest thoughts into his notes for tomorrow.

Section 3

A

Strategy

for

Winning

13

GOAL!

Chase had slept with the sliding glass door wide open, allowing the sound of the waves to lull him to sleep. He awoke feeling refreshed, yet anxious to continue his discussions with Coach Billings. This would be their last day together, and Chase wanted to make the most of it. Chase once again showered, dressed, grabbed his portfolios and headed down to Big Joe's a little past 7:30.

This time Chase arrived before Billings did, so Chase secured the same table they had used in their previous meetings. Chase considered it serendipitous that their table was one of only two that were not currently occupied. Coach arrived ten minutes later, happy to find Chase already there.

"Good to see you again Chase. I see you got here early this morning."

Chase shook Coach's hand as they greeted each other. "I remember that being on time for every meeting was one of the points on your Leadership Philosophy. It's one of my pet peeves as well, so I wasn't about to be late."

Coach laughed. "Good to hear. How was your evening?"

"It was good. I think I have some good stuff to share with you. I'm excited to hear your feedback."

"Well, let's order some breakfast and get started then, shall we?"

The gentlemen provided their breakfast meal choices to the same waitress who had served them the day before. Chase could tell that Coach was not one to waste much time, so he offered to share his thoughts and ideas on the topics they discussed the day before.

Coach was an attentive listener, and asked a few questions on some of Chase's ideas. Chase finished laying out his plan just as their breakfast arrived. When they were finished eating, Coach segued the conversation to the next topic he wanted to discuss.

"Those are some great ideas. I think they will work extremely well. I think you've got the good start to your Strategy for Winning."

"My Strategy for Winning?"

"Yep. Having great ideas is only the first step. The true test of leadership is implementing and maintaining those ideas, with the full support of your team. They have to buy into your vision, because they believe that you believe whole heartedly in what you are presenting to them. Today I'd like to talk about the key pieces of implementing a strategy successfully."

"That sounds great."

"Ok, this may sound strange, but let's start at the end. We talked a little about this the first day. You need to know where you are today, and where you want to be. In other words, you need to have a good idea of what success will look like. And more importantly, you will need to be able to tell if the strategy is working along the way."

"Coach, I'm assuming that you are talking about goals. I'm a big believer in setting goals."

"That's good to hear. Goals are such an important aspect to success. And when I talk about goals, I'm not just talking about the desired end state, but all of the important steps along the way. As an example, for me, success is not just winning the championship. Don't get me wrong, that is a big part of it, but there are other factors included in it than just the season record.

To me, when I'm setting goals, I need to include non-tangible things such as team chemistry, morale and job satisfaction. I also include ticket and merchandising revenue. I understand that these things are co-dependent on each other. Without good team chemistry, you won't win a lot of games, let alone a championship. Without a winning team, it's hard to sell tickets and merchandise.

Another important piece are goals regarding the development of your personnel. We talked yesterday about having development plans for each person, based on leveraging their strengths. I set goals for each of my team members, with their input. I then held them to meeting or exceeding those goals. I also consider having a member of my staff promoted as a level of success. Although I hate to lose someone, it allows them to follow their dreams, and opens up an opportunity for someone else to step in and be successful.

For each of these factors, I put together specific measurements of what level of success I want in each area, and when I want those levels to be met."

"I've made goals before Coach, but this will be the first time that I am responsible for the success of the entire organization. I need to make sure that I, along with my team, develop good goals that will enable us to make sure we are doing the right things, that we are heading in the right direction, and that we are doing it in the proper timeframe."

"I'm glad to hear you say that. In my world, when we are building goals, we use the **TEAM** Goal criteria. The acronym stands for Timely, Explicit, Achievable and Measurable. I know that many businesses use the SMART acronym, but for reasons I'm sure you can understand, I like TEAM better. Let me explain each of these.

Timely--The goal needs to clearly state when a specific criteria of the goal is to be met. If you don't have a timeframe associated with the desired state, then you won't know if you are on path to meet your goal within your strategy timeline, and there won't be any sense of urgency for the person to achieve their goal.

Explicit--The goal needs to be extremely specific as to what the expected result is to be attained. Don't leave anything to interpretation, or in other words, don't be vague.

Achievable--You want the goal to be something that can be achieved, but will require some level of growth or improvement in order to do so. Goals should not be lay-downs, as that doesn't help you, the individual, or your team. They also cannot be unattainable, far-fetched desires, or you will find that your team will not buy into the goals, your credibility will be hurt, and your team culture will be severely damaged.

Measureable--The goal needs to be developed so that the desired result can be measured. If you can't measure whether the outcome is at the level desired, then you can't tell if the goal was actually achieved or not. Also, when building your goal, make sure that the measurement is something that is easy to do. Don't make one that will require long analysis of different reports. Keep it simple."

"I really like that approach. The TEAM acronym really fits into the culture I want to develop. It can be a subliminal reminder as to the desired state, having the people think more about the overall team. Coach, I think I'll use it for all the goals we will be setting. Let me read my notes back to you to make sure I captured everything correctly, if you don't mind."

"Not at all."

Chase read back his notes on each of the four elements of

the goals. Coach added a little clarity wherever Chase was missing something, which was very understandable based on how fast Chase was forced to write while Coach was speaking.

When Chase was finished writing, Coach continued, "Chase, you can utilize this approach in your professional and your personal life. Make goals for yourself using the TEAM approach, and then work hard to attain those goals. You mentioned that you and Reagan are thinking about having your basement finished. This would be a great example of a TEAM goal. You can use it for virtually any goal that you have in your life."

"I love that idea. Everyone has things that they want to accomplish. Using this approach lets you keep them in focus, and can help you reach those goals faster than if you just put them on the back burner."

"Exactly."

14

Weekly Game Plan

"Chase, using the goal setting approach that we just discussed, you'll have the long term goals that reflect where the organization needs to get to, but you should also break it down into smaller pieces. For me, I do what I call a weekly game plan. In this, I lay out what my objectives are for the week, and again place TEAM goals against each objective. These are specific goals that I want to have completed, or at least to a certain state by the end of each week. I review my weekly game plan each morning to see how I've advanced on each goal, and what pieces I want or need to get accomplished that day."

"Would you use that same approach for goals that might take you a few weeks to complete?" Chase asked as he wrote notes.

"I would, but each week I would break down how far along I want to be on that particular goal. This way I break it down into Timely, Explicit, Achievable and Measurable pieces."

"I do something a little similar, but I really like your

approach to it. I'll add it to my list of things that I want to incorporate into my normal day-to-day activities."

"I also have each of my assistant coaches follow this same approach. I check in with them each week to see how they are progressing against their weekly game plans. It really helps keep our conversations focused on the important things we are addressing each week. We can discuss challenges they are having, celebrate successes when they meet their goals, etc. You might want to have your directors do this as well. It might give you a quicker insight into their world, what challenges they are facing, and help you evaluate their strengths."

"I agree. I am definitely going to do that. I wonder how much they are going to push back against these changes."

"Well, if they do, then you will need to make some tough decisions. You need a staff under you that buys into your vision. You can't have them contradicting you in front of the team members. You'll have to lay out that expectation right up front with them, and make sure they understand the consequences of doing so. Use your weekly meetings with them to make sure they are on-board with each piece. As long as you explain the reasoning behind each piece, and they fully understand it, they should support you one hundred percent. If they don't, then it may be time for you to play Free Agency."

"I understand. I would expect that you wouldn't be able to win a championship if your assistant coaches aren't following your philosophy. I can imagine how disruptive that would be to a team."

"Right again Chase, but I want to circle back on something you just mentioned, because we haven't talked about it yet and I told you yesterday that we would. You mentioned change, and how some people push back against it or resist it. I think it is extremely important for leaders to understand this, and also how to help their team members absorb the change quickly. The faster someone does this, the less amount of time and effort is wasted on non-productive worrying, rumors and resistance."

"Coach, I've lived through changes at work where it hasn't gone very well. In some cases, they ended up reverting back to the old way because they couldn't get everyone to accept the change. How do you help with that?"

"First, it is important to draw a mental picture of this process we go through. I would say that a good metaphor would be a roller coaster. Roller Coasters provide lots of sudden drops, twists, and turns. When you think about it, life is like a roller coaster. We all face numerous changes in our lives – some twists and turns, some ups and downs, some peaks and valleys that we contend with, sometimes on a daily basis. Not everyone likes to ride roller coasters and not everyone responds to them in the same way. When you ride one for the first time, you aren't sure exactly what to expect. This causes anxiety, a higher level in some people and less in others. Now, a roller coaster changes course with a series of ups and downs, just like life. Can you think of some examples of changes in your life that you would consider an up?"

"Sure, I mean getting married was a change, and I would definitely consider it an up. I know that when we have our first child, that will be an extreme change, but it will also be an up. I can also give you some examples of some changes that would be considered downs. Reagan's father passed away suddenly, a little more than a year ago. That was one of the worst downs I've ever had to live through."

"Chase, those are examples that almost anyone can relate to. Some changes in our lives are planned, while others are unexpected. Some changes are positive, while others are not. We react to these changes based on several things, such as the experiences we've had in our lives. We deal with changes throughout our life, however you can't expect every person to deal with change in the same way. When we have difficulty is when we don't understand why the change is happening. There is a normal process that people go through whenever change is thrust upon them. There are steps, or more like invisible phases to this process. The four steps are awareness, questioning, acceptance, and finally, normality. The faster you can get people through these phases, the quicker they accept the changed environment and will be back to their prior level of productivity, or higher."

"What do the different phases represent?"

"A person enters the awareness phase as soon as the changes are introduced or proposed. At this point, they don't know all the details, but they understand that a change will be occurring. Soon after this, they will enter the questioning phase. People question because they want to better understand. Once a person feels that their questions have been answered, they will move into the acceptance phase. At last, once they have been in this phase long enough, and the timing is different for everybody, they will move into the normality phase. The change that had occurred is now a part of their normal life or routine."

"I can understand that, but how do we help people through the phases?"

"One of the best ways is to communicate clearly and honestly. Make sure they understand why the change is being implemented, and how it fits into your vision for the company. Once a person understands the "why" behind the change, then they are quicker to move through the questioning phase and into the acceptance phase. They may not always agree one hundred percent, but they will move through the phases quicker. Also, make sure that you and your leadership team are speaking the same language, or that you are all on the same page. You can't be saying one thing while one of your directors is saying something different. Lastly, I would say that it is important to be persistent. If you believe the change is the right thing for the company, then stand behind it and see it through. Once you waffle, or backtrack on a change, then you will lose credibility and then you will have a much tougher time gaining acceptance for any future changes."

Chase was busy writing notes, so Coach sat silent for a minute while Chase finished. Finally, Chase looked up and said, "Coach, this is great stuff. I know that this will come in handy, as I have a good number of changes that I need to implement, and it will be important that the team gets to the normality phase as quickly as possible."

15

Know Your Opponent

"Chase, I'm going to change up the subject. Now I'm sure you've heard stories about how much film we watch of our upcoming opponents. Why do you think we do this?"

"That's an easy one. You want to know what they do in certain situations, what their trends are, how each of their people perform, etcetera. It allows you to formulate your plan on how you are going to exploit their weaknesses, and how you are going to stop them from scoring against you."

"Great explanation. I would assume that this would be just as important in your world. Am I correct?"

"Oh yes! If you aren't keeping an eye on your competition, you can be blindsided and lose a serious chunk of market share before you even knew what hit you. It would also be impossible to put together a strong marketing strategy if you didn't know how your products or services compare to the competition's. It's very similar to your world. Knowing your opponent, as you call it, is very important."

"I expected as much. Having heard you tell me how important it is to know your opponent, what can you tell me about your competition?"

Chase hesitated before stating, "Honestly Coach, not much at all. I may be completely wrong, but I don't think we have a very good grasp on what the competition is doing, or even more importantly how we are doing against them."

"Chase, seems like you and your team might have some serious work to get done in a short amount of time. I'm sure you've already figured out in your mind, but if you don't have a good understanding of your competition, or your opponent, then you're shooting blind. It is impossible to build a solid strategy for winning if you don't know how to compete strongly against your opponents."

"I can see that. I could imagine what would happen to your team if you didn't do your due diligence and know your opponent prior to facing them in a game."

"It wouldn't be pretty, and I can assure you that my team members wouldn't be too impressed with my leadership. It would also be safe to say that I probably wouldn't hold my position very long either. Now for me, I need to have a good understanding of each key player on the other team, but I also need to know how their coaches think and react in certain situations. What types of things would it be important for you to know about your competition?"

"Off the cuff, I can think of a few things. If you don't mind, I'd like to write them down as we talk so that I can remember each of them for later."

"Sounds like a good idea to me."

Chase began writing out each point as he brought them up.

1. Who is their management team made up of?

2. What is their current and past marketing messages?

3. How does their product or service differ from ours?

4. How does their delivery / customer service differ from ours?

5. How does their pricing structure differ from ours?

6. How does their professionalism match up to ours?

7. What is their current market share?

8. Has it grown or declined in the last six months? If so, why?

9. Has their staff size changed in the last six months? If so, why?

"Those are some great questions Chase, and they should really give you a good sense of your opponents. If I may make a suggestion, I would delegate this project to your directors. I do this with my assistant coaches, giving each of them responsibility for reporting on the opponent in their realm of responsibility. For example, have your Customer Service Director report on how the opponent's customer service differs from yours. They can use whatever resources are necessary to get the information, but they must present it back to you in a group presentation."

"I could see that serving several purposes. First, sharing the information in a group setting allows each of the directors to gain insight in the competition and may spur some very good ideas on how we can compete against them. Secondly, it will again allow me an opportunity to evaluate the proficiency of my directors."

"You're right. Now, once you have all this intelligence gathered, the next step is sharing this information with your entire team. Any thoughts on why I believe you should do this?"

"To me, it makes sense to share the information. It goes back to what you have been talking about; It's all about the team. The more you keep them informed the more engaged they will feel. I would also assume that it also ties into the having fun, since there isn't too many things more fun than beating your competition."

"That's right Chase. I can't think of too many feelings that are better than being a part of a winning team, whether it's in the sports world or in the business world. Now, it wouldn't do me much good to watch film and evaluate my opponent if I then didn't share that information with my team. After all, they are the ones that have to execute the strategy. Remember, communication is the key to successful change. Just like my players, your team members will more easily buy into your strategy for beating your opponent if they understand where you are coming from. What you will also discover is that some of your team members might step up with ideas of their own; ones that you can incorporate into the overall strategy."

"Coach, these are all great ideas, but should I be concerned that I'm trying to do too much in such a short amount of time? Couldn't the team get a little overwhelmed?"

"Chase, that is a great segue into the next topic I want to discuss with you. But first, I could go for some Iced Tea. You want some?"

"You bet."

16

The Power of Momentum

"Chase, why do you think leaders get fired?"

"Well, it could be for a couple of reasons; they did something to embarrass themselves or the company; they broke a law or a company policy; most likely though, they weren't doing a good job and the company wasn't heading in the right direction."

"I agree. From what you've told me, your situation falls in the latter category."

"Yep. The board made a change because sales and profits were falling. My job is to turn that around."

"My situations have been very similar. Normally a coach loses his job because the team's record isn't what the ownership expects, and they don't see things getting better without making a change."

"Coach, you've got me a little puzzled. We've been talking about how to build a winning team, and now we're talking about why people get fired."

"Bear with me for just a minute. You'll see where I'm heading. As I said, in most cases, a leader is removed because those above him or her don't believe that they have the right vision to lead the organization in the way they want it to, or that they aren't capable of leading the team to meet that vision. They will then replace that person with another leader, and they expect that person to turn the company around. Would you say that is a fair representation?"

"I hadn't really thought about it before, but yes, I guess I would agree with that statement. I'm sure that there are some folks that lose their leadership position because they did something wrong, such as breaking a rule or policy, but those would be rare. Most of the time they are removed because the company wasn't performing the way it was expected to."

"I'm glad you used that word--expected. Chase, we talked the first day about expectations. I asked you at that time what is expected of you?"

"I remember."

"So, circling back on that topic, and speaking in generalities, what is expected of you from the people that hired you, and also from those that report to you. What are their expectations of you?"

"I would say that they expect me to work hard and lead the organization to higher sales and profits. I would expect that it would be similar to when you are hired and take over a team. You are expected to win a championship. Is that not correct?"

"Oh sure, that is the end desire, but what I'm trying to get you to see is that you need to make sure that the expectations or goals that you set as part of your strategy are realistic. Remember the discussion we had about the formula S=P-E? Would it have been realistic for me to take the team from last place to winning the championship in just one year?"

"No, I would think that would be virtually impossible. There was probably a lot of things that needed to be addressed, and it will take some time to get everything working the way you want it to."

"That's right. So, what I need to do is have realistic expectations of myself and my team, and what we can accomplish in a certain amount of time. That doesn't mean that I'm not going to set goals that will require significant movement in the right direction, but not so far out there that they are unattainable. If the expectations are unrealistic, then it will be pretty much impossible to be successful. Do you see what I'm saying?"

"I do, and I think I see where you might be going with this. Tell me if this is along the lines you are thinking. I will be developing and sharing with everyone in the organization a strong vision of what the company can and should be. I will then build and implement a strategy to help us get there. As part of that strategy, I will be setting goals that will be used to track our progress. I need to make sure that the goals are set are moving us in the right direction, but are also realistic. Is that close to what you are looking for?"

Coach laughed. "That is exactly what I was looking for. As you set milestone dates for each piece of your strategy, make sure that they are realistic. I mentioned this before, but it bears mentioning again; you will lose all credibility and destroy any progress you might have made in building a winning team culture if you are asking for things that are not realistic. Your team will know it. Here's another suggestion for you; build your strategy with smaller, easier achievements in the front end. This way you will build momentum, which is extremely important."

"I like that idea Coach. Having some positive momentum

will really help the morale of the entire organization, and should help everyone with buying into my strategy."

"Chase, we talked earlier about Winning Attitudes, and how it is something that can't be measured. The same goes with momentum. It isn't something that can be tracked or measured, but you sure can tell that it is there. In the sports world, we know how powerful it can be. We want it on our side. In my experience, I have found that there are two reasons that someone gets motivated. The first is when their backs are up against the wall, such as when time is running out, or the other team is getting close to scoring. The second is when you feel that you are part of something positive, such as making great plays, or scoring in back to back opportunities."

"Coach, I think that is true in our personal lives as well. I know for a fact that it is true in business."

"I agree. As a coach, I'll try to build momentum by running plays that I know we can execute well. It helps the team get confidence, which in turn helps build momentum. I'll leverage my team leaders to help get the entire team fired up. I believe that you can do the same thing in your situation. When you are building your strategy, keep this in mind. Also, look for ways every day to build and feed the positive momentum. You'll see people step up and do things that even they weren't sure they could do. Celebrate the successes along the way, no matter how small they are. Everyone feeds off it, and it's fun."

"I see what you are saying. We've put together our strategy, and we have created specific TEAM goals to help us make sure we are heading in the right direction at the expected speed. As we meet these goals and milestones along the way, we should celebrate them. Also, since we know that communication is one of the keys, we make sure we let everyone know that we are hitting our goals, and that our plan for winning is working. Again Coach, this sounds like a no-brainer, but it isn't something that I have found commonly done in the business world. I can assure you that I will do this, as I see the benefits it will bring."

"You're right Chase. On my teams, we celebrate the little things, not just the superb plays that result in a score. Those scores are a result of the momentum we start by celebrating our smaller successes along the way. The same can happen in your business."

Chase took a few moments to write down some notes.

17

Make Adjustments

"All right Chase, we're winding down. How about we get up and take a walk. In my job, I'm on my feet most of the day. I'm not used to sitting for so long."

Coach Billings settled their bill from the breakfast and iced teas. They walked down the same path to the beach that they had used the first day they met. The benches were all being used this time by people enjoying the beautiful weather. Chase was happy that he had remembered to bring his sunglasses.

Coach let out a chuckle. "Looks like there's no place to sit down here. How about we keep walking. You ok with that?"

"Sure Coach. It's a gorgeous day for it."

"I was planning on grabbing one of those benches, but it plays right into the next thing I wanted to talk to you about. When I put together a strategy for a particular game we will be playing, there is bound to be some aspects that I didn't account for. After all, the coach for the other team has been doing the same thing I've been doing in preparing for the game. He's put together his strategy to take advantage of a weakness he believes he has found in our approach. When this happens, we need to make adjustments. We need to make modifications on the fly to address the current situation. Does this make sense to you?"

"Sure Coach. I believe It happens in every sport. In baseball, the manager may need to send in a relief pitcher earlier then they had planned because the starter isn't being effective. In football, everyone's heard about half-time adjustments. In hockey, the coach may change up the lines. I'm sure there are examples you could pull from virtually every other sport as well."

"I agree. Now, why do you think we all do this? Why is it so important that we make these adjustments during a game?"

"Coach, that seems like it might be a trick question, because the answer is so obvious. They make adjustments because they are now facing situations that they didn't anticipate, and the adjustments give them the best chance to win the game."

"You're right, and it wasn't a trick question. But here's what puzzles me Chase, if it is so obvious that making adjustments is so vital in the world of sports, why doesn't it happen more in business?"

"Now that is a good question, and I don't think I can give you an answer. I know what you are talking about though. It seems that most businesses will put together a strategy, but then will hold to that same strategy. They may not even know if it is working like they were hoping it would, but they still keep plodding along. I know that there are a handful of businesses that do a good job of adjusting their strategy, and those are most likely the companies that are winning the battle for market share."

"Chase, they are winning the game of business. Make no mistake, the fight for market share among companies is very similar to sports teams battling each other, it just that we keep score in different ways. We put points on the board and try to gain as many loyal fans as possible. You gain market share and try to build up your loyal customer base. To win the game you need to have a good strategy, but don't forget that your strategy needs to be fluid."

"I understand what you are saying. I think I can give you an example; if our major competitor changes something in their business that they think will allow them to grab some of our market share, then we need to be able to identify it and adjust our strategy as quickly as possible."

"Right, and what would happen if you didn't adjust in a timely manner?"

"Well, if the adjustments they made work, then we could lose customers, which means lower revenue and less profits. Coach, it's very likely that this is one of the reasons that my company is in the situation it is in. The founder did a great job getting the company up and running, but I think he was stuck in that strategy, and it finally caught up with him. He, nor the company, made the adjustments necessary not only to keep their existing business, but also to continue growing the business."

"The good news Chase is that the competition might have won a few games, but the season isn't over by a long shot. In fact, your season never ends. You have an opportunity to right the ship, to build a winning team, and to win every one of the remaining games."

"I got you Coach. Build a solid strategy, but make adjustments along the way as necessary to put you in the best situation to win."

"Exactly! And here's another hint for you. Feed off the intelligence around you. You're people will tell you what is going on in the marketplace. You need to make sure you personally thank a team member when they come to you with information that can help you win. My players will come to me, or one of the other coaches and let us know what the other team is doing against them. They know that if they bring us this intelligence, we can make adjustments to our strategy to put us in a better position to win. Your team members will do the same, as long as they feel the information is being accepted and acted upon."

"Coach, I will definitely incorporate that into our culture. I can see how someone in sales, customer service or shipping might be able to gain some information on a competitor that we might not have known about otherwise. Heck, the information could come from anywhere, and we need to be able to take it, analyze it, and use it to our advantage."

"Good, now I suggest we turn around and head back to the resort. I didn't realize we had walked so far."

18

Sports Talk Junkies

The two men turned around, heading back towards the resort. The beach was full of people relaxing, families enjoying their vacation, and sun worshipers adding another shade of bronze to their skin. A light coastal breeze made the warm weather very comfortable.

"Chase, we've talked about a good number of situations that are similar between your world and mine. There are a few things that are a little different that I think you need to also be aware of."

"You mean besides the difference between my salary and yours?" Chase joked.

Coach laughed. "Yes. In my world when my customers, our fans, are not happy with something they have an outlet to vent their opinions and frustrations. They call the local sports talk stations and let their thoughts be known. They will talk to other fans, and have back and forth discussions as to why they believe we are doing a good job, or a bad job. Now, granted our fans might be a little more passionate and vocal than your customers, but that doesn't make them less important."

"That's definitely true in Philly. I listen to one of the sports talk stations every morning and afternoon. They sure can let you and the other coaches have it every once and a while."

"Chase, I understand that it comes with the territory, and I wouldn't have it any other way. Having passionate fans is a good thing, and I love them, but the key thing is when they question a decision that I made, or the performance of one of my team members. As our customer, they have every right to do so. Just remember that your customers will also question decisions you make that affect them. But it is harder for you to hear what they are saying. Now I'm not saying that every fan or person that calls into the radio show is right, sometimes it's far from it, but they are our customers, so it is important to understand how they feel."

"I hear you. I think that we need to take the steps necessary to keep our eyes and ears on the pulse of our customers. I think we can do that a few different ways. My first thought would be to do some type of formal customer survey to really get an idea of what they think about us. I'd also like to see us utilize some of the new social media platforms to get immediate feedback from our clients. Maybe it could be something like our own sports-talk outlet, where our customers could let us know of things they like and don't like. Our marketing department should be able to do something along those lines. In addition, I want to sit down with each of our major customers to get their input on how we are doing, and how we could do better."

"It might also be worthwhile to find out if you have lost any clients recently, and talk to them. It would be helpful to find out exactly why they stopped doing business with you."

"That's true. It must be something we did, something we didn't do, or something that our competition offered them, most likely. Finding out exactly what happened to cause us to lose their business would be great information. We might even be able to win some of that business back."

"I agree Chase." Coach Billings paused. "I've got a confession to make, but I want you to keep it to yourself. We do try and listen to what our customers are saying. I have people within the organization that monitor what the public is saying. Sometimes they have some great ideas that we can leverage. At minimum our marketing department makes sure that our website is full of content that provides or customers information about decisions we make, in regards to team members and our overall strategy. My coaching staff, the players and even I will conduct interviews with radio and television hosts in order to communicate with our fans. The better informed we can keep our customers, or our fans, the more they feel engaged. This is the same approach I take with my team members. I make sure they are all aware of a decision before it hits the streets."

"I take the same approach Coach. And I think it's a key aspect of Change Leadership which we discussed earlier. It will be extremely important in my new role, as it looks like I'll be instituting a good amount of change over the next few months."

"I agree. It's key for every leader to be well versed in change leadership. Getting your team members to buy into your strategy and the changes that go along with it will be vital to your success. We've talked about a good number of important aspects to change and leading teams. I'd like to hear your ideas on how you are going to lead your team though the change."

"First is to share out the key reasons and facts as to why the change is necessary. I will then set the expectations that we will be implementing a new strategy to address our situation and get us headed in the direction we need to. As we roll out each piece, I'll make sure I have key people within the organization help in sharing the information with the rest of the team. Having it come from their peers will help them buy into the changes. We need to keep everyone informed and not let any rumors start. We also need to make sure that the work environment is fun, as this will help people adapt to the changes. Finally, we need to foster an environment of sharing information, as the intelligence we can gather from our team members will allow us to make necessary adjustments or changes in our strategy quickly and effectively."

"I think that is a great way to approach it. Change is inevitable, especially when you are trying to build a winning team. You'll also need to make decisions along the way to maintain a winning team after you get there. There will be change associated with that as well, as your competition will adjust and the overall market will change.

Chase, we make decisions that affect changes in our lives every day. From something as simple as getting a new haircut, to buying a different car, to the extreme when we make changes in our personal relationships. The key is to make those decisions based on the best information you can gather. This increases your likelihood of those decisions improving your situation, whether at work or in your personal life."

"Much like my decision to spend time with you this week instead of sitting in the seminar that I was originally here to attend. I know that it has had a positive effect on my life."

"I appreciate that Chase. I've really enjoyed our conversations, and I'm confident that you will be successful in building a winning team. What do you say we go back into Big Joe's, grab some lunch, and talk about your next steps. I also need to get your e-mail address so that I can send you that information I promised. We can then call it a day."

"Sounds good to me. I want one last burger from Big Joe's before I leave tomorrow."

"I know what you mean."

Chase and Coach Billings walked the short distance remaining to Big Joe's. Once they were back at a table, Chase wrote down notes on the topics they had discussed during their walk, getting some help from Coach to make sure he had captured everything. The two men also exchanged contact information.

"I'd like for you to keep me updated on your progress. Perhaps you and your wife would like to come to a game as my guest? I'm assuming she is a fan also?"

"She's even more crazy about sports than I am. We'd love to come. I think I'm going to be pretty busy for the next few months, but we need to keep a good balance between our work and personal lives, right?"

"You're right. Of course you know that I'm an extreme workaholic, but I always find time to spend with my family and for the great charities that I'm privileged to be a part of. I've got a good feeling that you are going to do great in your new role. Just take some time to put together your plan on how you are going to implement the things we've talked about. Doing it right is better than doing it fast. Some other last advice; leverage the people around you. Utilize your directors and other people within the organization. You'll be able to tell who you can rely on in a short amount of time. Have confidence in your strategy, but remember to be willing to make adjustments along the way. And lastly, don't hesitate to reach out to me if you are having any problems. Think of me as your leadership coach."

"Coach, I can't thank you enough for the great information you've given me. I'm really looking forward to getting back this next week and starting to build my winning team."

"As they say, Chase... let the games begin."

The legendary coach and his newest disciple ate a delicious lunch, then bid each other a safe trip home. Chase returned to his room, anxious to start putting his strategy together.

He worked for the rest of the afternoon and evening in his room, taking a short break to grab a quick bite for dinner at Big Joe's. He was able to say goodbye to Big Joe, who, as usual, was making sure each of his clients that evening were enjoying themselves.

The tables were occupied by a good number of people that had been attending the leadership seminar. Chase purposely eavesdropped on a few of the conversations. The overall sentiment is that the entire meeting had been a bust. The keynote speaker that day had been entertaining, but didn't really share anything that was groundbreaking or inspiring. Chase felt a little sorry for each of these people. In his opinion, he had received the best leadership advice a person could get. He hoped that someday, if he was successful in implementing the lessons he had received, that he would be able to pass the information along to others.

Chase called Reagan, updating her on his conversation with Coach. He wasn't sure which she was more excited about, the things that Chase had learned from Coach, or his offer to see a game as his guest.

Chase once again checked his e-mail, sending off a message to his directors in which he asked them to meet first thing Monday morning, and to clear their calendars from nine until noon Tuesday, Wednesday and Thursday. He then packed up his clothes. He wanted to be ready to head to the airport first thing in the morning.

He was anxious to get home and see Reagan, but also to get back to work on Monday. As he finally laid down to sleep, he remembered something Coach had said earlier...

Chase repeated the words to himself, "That's right, let the games begin!"

Section 4

Let The

Games

Begin!

19

A Plan Comes Together

Chase had spent most of the weekend fine-tuning his strategy, and his agenda for the Monday morning director's meeting. Reagan had reviewed the strategy and helped him make sure Chase had incorporated all of the topics that Coach had discussed with her husband. As they reviewed each topic, Chase would look back over his notes, recounting the discussions once again for Reagan's benefit.

Monday morning finally arrived. Chase was surprised at how well he had slept the night before. He had anticipated a restless night, but he had slept well. His drive into work was another matter. He found himself to be increasingly anxious. This meeting had to go well. He had to get the buy-in of the directors. He was completely confident that the strategy was the right one. It was up to him to share the details properly so that the directors would also see the validity of the approach. Chase walked into the building at 7am, an hour before anyone else was scheduled to arrive. Chase was pleasantly surprised when his assistant, Ellen, showed up a little past 7:30. She helped Chase make copies of the different documents he wanted to cover with the directors. When Chase walked into the conference room a few minutes before eight, the six directors were already there, seated around the large wood table. Kevin, the customer service director sat on one side between Lisa, the director over the sales department and Fred, who oversaw the accounting department. On the opposite side of the table sat Tom, the leader of the marketing department, Kristin, who led the human resources department, and Brad, who ran the shipping department.

Chase greeted each of them and then kicked things off, "Let me start by thanking each of you for clearing your calendar this week and meeting with me this morning. I have some information that I want to share with you that I think is critically important. As everyone knows, our sales and profit results have been anything but spectacular. I firmly believe that we have the ability to turn this around, but it is going to take a team effort to do so. When I say team effort, I'm talking about every single person in the organization. That's me, you, and every associate we have here that makes up our team. In this meeting, I want to share with you my strategy for building a winning team. Your input into the details, and your support of this strategy is vital to its success, as the team members will be looking to each of you for leadership.

Before I dive in, I want to draw a parallel between where we are and where one of our local sports teams recently found themselves. As you know, we hadn't seen a championship in this town in quite a while. The team members played hard, but there was something, or maybe a few things missing that kept them from being consistent winners. They recently made some changes in their leadership, who brought with him a change in philosophy. This leader's fellow coaches bought into that philosophy, and soon so did the team members. They didn't completely overhaul the organization. They made slight changes in their approach, or their strategy, which caused huge improvements in morale and the overall culture. I don't have to tell you that they exceeded everyone's expectations this last season. I sincerely believe that we can do the same thing here. With the right strategy, we can turn this organization around and build a Winning Team environment. Let me walk through the different points, and I welcome your questions as we discuss each area. It is important that you fully understand the reasoning behind the strategy if you are going to help implement its concepts. What do you say, shall we begin?"

Three of the directors gave an enthusiastic response. Brad,

Fred and Lisa seemed to be hesitant to get too excited. Chase realized that they would take a little longer to get through the change phases, and he would have to help them along so that they could progress to the acceptance phase as quickly as possible.

As Chase walked through the details of his strategy, Tom, Kristin and Kevin asked good questions and filled the room with energy. As the conversation progressed, Fred and Brad became actively engaged and offered up their thoughts and ideas. Lisa, on the other hand, asked questions and made comments, but they were not supportive ones. Chase was happy to see Fred and Brad move past the questioning phase, but he was concerned with Lisa's lack of progression.

When Chase got to the topic of the company's Slogan of Purpose, the conversation was lively. Chase could tell that the directors had actually put some thought into it since his e-mail had been received. They were able to pull together a version that they all supported. Lisa's attitude seemed to change for the better during this part of the meeting. Chase hoped it would continue.

Chase took good notes of the different feedback and ideas that the directors came up with. The team was developing some great ideas on how to incorporate the key strategic points into the organization. Chase could feel some momentum building.

Chase brought up another item on his agenda. "I want to set up meetings with each of your departments this Friday. I'd like for each of you to be there as well. I will be sharing out my Leadership Philosophy, so that you and every person in the organization will understand what I believe in, what they can expect from me and what I will be expecting from each of them. I think we should be able to do it in a half hour each. Can each of you get that set up for your teams? I'd like to get these done this week."

Chase looked around the table to quickly gauge the reaction to his request. Overall the reactions seemed to be positive. "The sales team isn't going to like giving up a half-hour of selling time. They each have quotas they have to make," Lisa interjected.

"Lisa, They will need to find time. If you need to , bring in lunch and we'll do a working lunch. That way they won't lose selling time. Whatever it takes to get everyone together. Sound ok?"

Fred added his thoughts, "Lisa, your team won't mind a free lunch. I can attest to that based on their expense reports." Kristin spoke up as well, "We all need to be onboard, singing the same tune. We can all get our groups together this Friday, can't we?" Lisa and the other five directors agreed to schedule the meetings.

As the morning's meeting wrapped up, Chase committed to updating the strategy document and getting it back out to each of them. "I appreciate the input each of you gave during today's meeting. You have some great ideas, and I feel confident that together, we can lead this team to a great turnaround and once again become the leaders in the industry. I look forward to meeting with you over the next few days as we develop the details of the strategy." Chase also committed to putting a meeting on the calendar that would be attended by the entire staff. At this meeting, he and the directors would share out the strategy for turning the company around.

Chase asked Lisa to stay behind for a minute as everyone was getting up to leave the conference room. Chase closed the door so that they would have privacy. His conversations with Coach Billings had prepared him for what he needed to say.

"Lisa, I know that we have not worked together, and that I am coming in under a situation that isn't the most pleasant, but I need to know that each of my directors is fully committed to my vision for this company, and will be supportive of the strategy we roll out. I'm getting the feeling that you may not be there, and I want to address it with you right away. Am I seeing something that maybe isn't there?"

"Chase, I'm not one to beat around the bush. You ask me a question, I'm going to give you a straight answer."

"I appreciate that. I'm the same way."

"I've been here since the company opened, and worked my way up into this position. It's no secret that I'm not happy with the way things have happened here recently. I have nothing against you, but I don't think that they should have let Shawn go the way they did. In my opinion, he was one of the best bosses I've ever had. I hope that you will turn out to be one as well, but I can't sit here and put a smile on my face when I'm concerned about so many things. I hope you can respect that."

"I can respect that you feel that way, but I feel I need to be completely honest with you and everyone else here. No matter what has happened in the past, we are where we are. What I need now are leaders, people that will step up and help me take this company to the level it should be. I do not need people who are going to take a wait and see approach. To me, that isn't leading. What I want you to do is to think about what I've just said, and let's talk again tomorrow morning. Does that sound fair?"

"It does. But I hope you will remember that this is a sales driven organization. Without a good sales group bringing in customers, the business won't survive for long. Mr. Dunning, with all due respect, if you don't need me for anything else, I need to see how things are going in my department."

Chase was irritated with her blatantly condescending tone and use of his last name. Chase responded firmly, "Lisa, every single department and person here is important to our success, not just your sales team. We are all one team. We win together, or we lose together, and I don't intend on losing. I will not hesitate to make changes I feel need to be made in order to make sure we win. Other than that, I don't have anything else for you right now, and I hope I've made myself clear. Now, I hope the rest of your day goes well."

"Thanks." With that, Lisa got up and abruptly left the room.

Chase was pleasantly surprised with how he had handled

the situation. He thought to himself that if he hadn't met and talked with Coach Billings, then he would have allowed Lisa to continue with her behavior instead of addressing it head on. He knew instantly that Lisa would have to conform quickly, or he would have to take action. He hoped that she would come around.

Over the next few days, Chase and the six directors met to develop the details for each of the elements of their new strategy. They assigned ownership of tasks as well as deadlines. They worked to develop an exhaustive list of public touch-points for the Professionalism Manifesto. They discussed and agreed on new recruiting approaches to take advantage of Free Agency. Chase introduced the TEAM approach to goals, which the group then used to develop a new personal development program focused on a member's strengths. The group developed ideas for motivational materials as well as recognition and reward programs. The marketing team would start working on these as soon as the strategy was announced. Overall, they accomplished a great amount of work in a short amount of time. Chase was very pleased with their effort.

Lisa never seemed to fully buy in to the proposed changes. Chase engaged in further conversations with her in an attempt to bring her on board. At the same time, he worked with Kristin to start recruiting for a replacement, if that was eventually needed.

The meetings with the individual teams that Friday went extremely well. Chase, along with the directors introduced the overall strategy to the entire organization that next week. The games had begun.

20

Updating the Score

Five months had passed since Chase had the serendipitous meeting with Coach Billings. Chase and his wife, Reagan, had just watched their favorite team win from the comfort of the team luxury suite. They had been surprised at the will-call window when their tickets had been handed to them. They hadn't expected to sit in one of the suites, particularly the team suite. Most of the fans had already filed out of the stadium. Coach Billings had left a note with their tickets, asking them to stay so that he could come by and say hello. They waited for a good thirty minutes while Coach finished up his press conference. He entered the suite and immediately approached Chase and Reagan.

"Good to see you again Chase." Coach patted Chase's right shoulder as he gripped his hand and shook. Coach turned slightly towards the woman on Chase's left. "I assume this is your lovely wife; Reagan, if I remember correctly." Chase extended his hand to Reagan, who blushed while she took his hand. They shook. "Great to finally meet you in person."

"The pleasure is all mine Coach Billings. I can't thank you enough for the help you provided my husband."

"It was nothing, and please call me Don, or just plain old Coach. I hope you enjoyed the game?"

"It was great! Thanks again Coach for inviting us. It's so nice to see the team win another one. They really are playing well."

"Yep, it's truly a glorious thing to see a team perform. Chase, so tell me how things are going with your team. Based on some of your recent e-mails, it sounds like they are really coming together."

"Coach, I can't believe how far we've come in a relatively short amount of time. Overall the team really responded to the new direction. I did make a change in one of the directors, Lisa, who ran the sales department. She just couldn't seem to get on board of the whole team concept. I started looking into Free Agents right away and was able to fill her position very quickly. The new person is doing great and is a much better fit with our team environment. Our sales have flattened out, and I'm excited to see our figures for this month. I believe we are going to see our first gain in revenue. The whole team is going to celebrate."

"That's great! So it sounds like you are starting to win the game of leadership, and your team is really responding to your strategy."

"We are, and I owe it all to you. I don't know where the team would be right now if I hadn't met you and been privileged enough to gain so much insight from our conversations."

"No Chase, all I did was give you a little coaching. Just like my players today, it was you and your team that did all the hard work. Remember, one of the biggest responsibilities of a leader is to constantly coach the members of your team to improve themselves. You do that, as well as holding them to a high level of performance, and you'll continue to do well."

The two men stayed in close contact over the next several years. Coach Billings led his team to the playoffs each year, winning an unprecedented fourth championship. Chase and Reagan were guests at the celebration for that championship. Chase, following the strategy he developed from Coach's initial advice, was able to completely turn the company around. Sales, profits and morale were much higher. The winning team environment, which took a short while to take hold, is now the culture. It is a fun and fulfilling place to work.

Almost three years to the date that Chase met Coach Billings in Big Joe's Tropical Oasis, the two men were there once again sharing a delicious breakfast.

"So Chase, are you ready for today?"

"Yes. I have been practicing for weeks. Reagan has really helped in getting me ready."

"Well then, we should probably be going."

The two friends settled their bill and walked towards the conference rooms. Chase was today's keynote speaker at the Billings Team Leadership Seminar, which was at full capacity. Unlike the last seminar Chase had witnessed here, these attendees, made up of both sports and business leaders, were fully engaged and enjoying the seminar. The information they were receiving would benefit each of them, allowing them to gain the insights and skills to build winning teams in their organizations.

Section 5

Important

Documents

21

E-mails from Coach

As promised, Coach Billings sent Chase a few e-mails which contained a variety of pertinent quotes and stories. Chase was able to leverage many of these into the motivational materials his marketing department developed.

The entire team was very receptive and appreciative of the ongoing focus on teamwork. It also helped foster a fun environment, which led to the expected reduction in turnover, and a substantial increase in productivity.

To: Chase Dunning

From: Don Billings

Subject: Leadership Quotes

Chase, below you will find the leadership quotes I promised. I hope that you will be able to find use for them. I know I have over the years. Good Luck to you and your team!

Coach Billings

Leadership

Leadership is getting people to work for you when they are not obligated.

Fred Smith

A real leader faces the music, even when he doesn't like the tune.

Anon

Effective leadership is not about making speeches or being liked;

leadership is defined by results not attributes Peter Ferdinand Drucker

Win!

Leadership is getting someone to do what they don't want to do, to achieve what they want to achieve Tom Landry

Leadership is action, not position Donald H. McGannon

The first responsibility of a leader is to define reality. Max DePree

If you are failing to plan, you are planning to fail. Tariq Siddique

Sometimes, the hardest decision made is the right thing to do.... Yanny Natashah

The vision must be followed by the venture. It is not enough to stare up the steps - we must step up the stairs. Vance Havne

Define your business goals clearly so that others can see them as you do. George F. Burns

The measure of success is not whether you have a tough problem to deal with, but whether it's the same problem you had last year. John Foster Dulles

The country is full of good coaches. What it takes to win is a bunch of interested players. Don Coryell

I won't accept anything less than the best a player's capable of doing... and he has the right to expect the best that I can do for him and the team! Lou Holtz

If anything goes bad, I did it. If anything goes semi-good, then we did it. If anything goes really good, then you did it. That's all it takes to get people to win football games. Paul "Bear" Bryant

Win!

To: Chase Dunning

From: Don Billings

Subject: Teamwork Quotes

Chase, I dug up my favorite teamwork quotes. I know that you can use these as you build your Winning Team.

Coach Billings

Teamwork

The whole is greater than the sum of the parts. Unknown

When a team outgrows individual performance and learns team confidence, excellence becomes a reality Joe Paterno

The era of the rugged individual is giving way to the era of the team player. Everyone is needed, but no one is necessary. Bruce Coslet

The strength of the team is each individual member...the strength of each member is the team. Phil Jackson

Talent wins games, but teamwork and intelligence wins championships. Michael Jordan

People who work together will win, whether it be against complex football defenses, or the problems of modern society. Vince Lombardi

Individual commitment to a group effort — that is what makes a team work a company work, a society work, a civilization work. Vince Lombardi

In order to have a winner, the team must have a feeling of unity; every player must put the team first-ahead of personal glory. Paul Bear Bryant

Gettin' good players is easy. Gettin' 'em to play together is the hard part. Casey Stengel

The achievements of an organization are the results of the combined effort of each individual. Vince Lombardi

If a team is to reach its potential, each player must be willing to subordinate his personal goals to the good of the team. Bud Wilkinson

All winning teams are goal-oriented. Teams like these win consistently because everyone connected with them concentrates on specific objectives. They go about their business with blinders on; nothing will distract them from achieving their aims. Lou Holtz

The important thing to recognize is that it takes a team, and the team ought to get credit for the wins and the losses. Successes have many fathers, failures have none. Philip Caldwell

Ask not what your teammates can do for you. Ask what you can do for your teammates. Magic Johnson

To: Chase Dunning

From: Don Billings

Subject: Inspirational Story

Chase, Here's one of my favorite stories about never giving up! Hope you can use it. You are on your way to Winning!!

Coach Billings

I know of a man that had failure look him in the eye on numerous occasions, but he never let it keep him from his desire to win.

Some of the failures this man endured:

- *He failed in his business at the age of 31*
- *He lost a legislative race at the age of 32*
- *He failed once again in business at the age of 34*
- *He dealt with the death of his sweetheart at the age of 36*
- *He lost an election at the age of 38*
- *He lost congressional races at the ages of 43, 46 and 48*
- *He lost in his bid to be Senator twice, at the ages of 55 and 58*

He finally won at the age of 60, elected as the 16th President of the United States.

His name was Abraham Lincoln

22

The Team Leadership Pledge

During each of the department meetings, Chase presented the Team Leadership Pledge. He made sure that copies were made for each person. He handed the copies out, and then went over each point making sure that everyone understood them.

Chase received nothing but positive feedback from the team members. They appreciated him being so up front and honest about what it was he was looking for, and how he was going to lead the organization.

Chase keeps a laminated copy of the document hanging in his office as a constant reminder to his commitment to his team members.

My Leadership Pledge

I, Chase Dunning, do hereby pledge to each of our team members,

that I will direct myself in accordance with the following principles

- I will give 100% towards the success of this team. I expect each of you to do the same.
- We are all human, and we will make mistakes. I vow to learn from each of mine, and I expect you to do the same.
- There will be times when I need to make tough decisions, which will impact some or all of you. When I do, I will try my best to make sure you understand my reasoning.
- I will be honest with you in all matters. In exchange, when I ask you for your input, I expect you to be honest with me, even if the news is bad.
- I will represent this organization in a professional manner. I expect each of you to do the same.
- I will not tolerate gossip, or the spreading of rumors. It adds no value to our team.
- I will be on time to every meeting. I expect each of you to do the same.
- If a team member needs my help, I will provide it. I expect each of you to do the same.
- If I have an idea that may help the team, I will raise it, no matter how crazy it may seem. I expect each of you to do the same.
- Don't be a problem spreader; Be a problem solver. Come to the table with proposed solutions.
- As conditions change, we may need to make adjustments to our strategy. I will be open to this and I expect you to be as well.
- I will not tolerate a team member being disrespected. I expect the same from you.
- I will not tolerate any breach in ethical behavior. If you are caught doing so, I will fire you. It's as simple as that.
- You will be given clear and specific goals. I expect each of you to work towards exceeding each of your goals. I will be doing the same.
- I will work to make this place a fun and enjoyable one. I need and expect your help in doing so.
- If I need help on something, I will ask for it. I need each of you to do the same.
- I will strive to build an environment of learning and advancement. I expect you to strive to learn new skills.

23

Strategy for Winning

After a good amount of input from team members, Chase was able to develop and roll out the strategy that the organization would follow.

The strategy was rolled out to everyone in an all-hands meeting two weeks after Chase had met Coach Billings.

The strategy was a huge success, helping to meet each of Chase's key objectives.

- Develop a Fun, Team Environment
- Develop and Maintain a Winning Attitude
- Develop the Skills of every Team Member
- Exceed the Expectations of Our Customers
- Win the Game of Business.

The strategy is still followed to this day.

Our Team's Strategy

In order to ensure the long-term success of our organization, we, as a team, will utilize the following strategy to guide our decisions and behaviors.

Slogan of Purpose

We are more than just a business. We are here to improve the lives of our customers by providing quality and effective products that exceed their expectations.

Leadership Pledge

We will each direct ourselves in accordance with the expected behaviors documented on our Leadership Pledge. As we are all leading this company to great heights, the Leadership Pledge is applicable to every team member within the organization. We have an inert ability to choose our reactions to each and every situation. We will choose actions that align with our pledged behaviors.

Standing Above the Competition

In order to set ourselves apart and above the competition, we will diligently ensure that every aspect of our organization is conducted in the most professional manner. This includes every possible public touch-point, as well as how we treat our fellow team members.

Success = Performance - Expectations

We will not be successful if the performance of our team is not greater than the expectations of our customers. We will do everything within our collective power to ensure that the expectations of every one of our customers is met.

Our Talent is our Team

We recognize that in order to win, we must leverage the great resource of talent that makes up our team. To do so, we will identify each team member's strengths, and help them further develop them utilizing personal developmental programs. We will require excellence in each and every one of our team members.

In addition, to continue the growth of talent, we will actively recruit quality team members on an ongoing basis. To help attract talent, we will initiate a team member referral program

Together We Win

We understand that the successful execution of this strategy is dependent on the synergy found only when all team members work towards a common goal. In acknowledgement of this fact, we understand and recognize the importance of every single position and team member within the organization.

Winning Will Be Fun

We will strive to build and maintain a safe and professional, yet fun work environment for all team members.

Going for the Goals

To ensure the effectiveness of our execution of this strategy, we will implement specific team and individual goals. These goals will follow the T.E.A.M concept, ensuring that they are Timely, Explicit, Achievable and Measurable. These goals will be developed to drive improvements throughout the organization.

Knowing our Opponents

We are aware that we are not the only ones in this game that want to win it. In order to compete against and beat our competition, every team member must be vigilant in collecting intelligence that can be leveraged in our pursuit to be successful. This intelligence will be gathered in any and every ethical and lawful way, and will be shared throughout the entire team.

Remaining Flexible

Although we have a great deal of faith and belief in the strategy that has been developed, we realize that conditions may change, and/or situations may arise that were not foreseen. To accommodate this, we resolve to remain flexible, making adjustments to our strategy in a timely manner whenever necessary, allowing us to continually have the best game plan of anyone in our industry.

24

Professionalism Manifesto

Chase and the directors completed and initiated the team's Professionalism Manifesto the same day he held the all hands meeting. The Manifesto included a checklist of every single potential public touch-point. Chase understood the importance of building and maintaining the company's brand in the marketplace, or how the company was perceived by its customers, both current and future, and the competition.

Every touch-point on the Professionalism Manifesto is revisited at the beginning of every month to ensure they are doing their best in each area. The results of each month's review are shared with the entire team, helping make sure the focus is vigilant.

Our Professionalism Manifesto

Maintaining a strong brand helps us compete against our competition in the marketplace, increases our customer base, and improves customer loyalty. Most importantly, it is a direct reflection of our business.

The following items must be reviewed on a monthly basis. Any areas of concerns should be brought to light immediately so that they can be addressed:

1. Is our standardized logo being used in every application?
2. Are our standardized colors being used in every marketing application?
3. Is every team member utilizing a standard signature on their work e-mail?
4. Is our key business phrase present on all applicable materials?
5. Is every phone answered in a consistent, professional manner?
6. Is every team member's voicemail message professional?
7. Does the quality of our newsletters and other written materials match our branding strategy?

8. Are our marketing materials written and/or proofread by a professional?

9. Does every one of our advertising messages meet our expected level of professionalism?

10. Is our website updated with current and relevant content?

11. Is our building exterior and interior clean, organized and welcoming?

12. Is the experience of our customers consistently pleasant?

13. Are our company vehicles clean?

14. Are our team members well groomed and dressed appropriately?

15. Do our team members know our marketing strategy?

About the Author

David Akers is the Founder and President of Akers Consulting Group, LLC. Mr. Akers started this boutique consulting organization, leveraging his more than twenty years of professional experience, in a quest to help businesses overcome their unique challenges to success. You can learn more about the many professional services offered by Akers Consulting Group, LLC at their website: http://www.AkersConsultingGroup.com

Mr. Akers is a recognized expert in business and process improvement, strategy, training, team development, change management, marketing and leadership. Akers' education includes a Bachelor's Degree in Business from Western Governors University, as well as a Master Certificate in Strategic Organizational Leadership from Villanova University.

Mr. Akers has developed and led numerous high-performing and winning teams in his career. He and many of his team members have received prestigious awards for their performance, and Mr. Akers has been the recipient of several awards for his leadership.

Originally born and raised in California, Mr. Akers now resides in a suburb of Philadelphia, PA along with his wife of 24 years and their teenage daughter. They are also the proud parents of two sons that are serving in the U.S. Marines.

Winning Team Systems

Building a winning team can be accomplished, if you have the right approach, strategy and focus. Having proven tools at your disposal is extremely important, and can make the difference between successfully building a winning team, or having a dysfunctional one.

To help support you in your endeavor to build a winning team, Winning Team Systems has collected a large number of tools and articles and have made them available to current and aspiring team leaders.

Discover materials that Coach Billings would have used in the Billings Team Leadership Seminar.

Visit the Winning Team Systems website, where you will find a large library of information, tools and strategies for building and being part of winning teams.

http://winningteamsystems.com

**Look for our newest book
in the
Winning Team Systems
catalogue**

Winners!

A Team-Members Guide to
being part of a Winning Team

Available fall of 2010.